DUBLIN

TOP SIGHTS • LOCAL EXPERIENCES

FIONN DAVENPORT

Contents

Plan Your Trip 4

Herbert Park (p139)
DAVID SOANES PHOTOGRAPHY / GETTY IMAGES ©

COVID-19

We have re-checked every business in this book before publication to ensure that it is still open following the COVID-19 outbreak. However, the economic and social impacts of COVID-19 will continue to be felt long after the outbreak has been contained, and many businesses, services and events referenced in this guide may experience ongoing restrictions. Some businesses may be temporarily closed, have changed their opening hours and services, or require bookings; some unfortunately could have closed permanently. We suggest you check with venues before visiting for the latest information.

Special Features

Dublin's Top Experiences

ANTON_IVANOV / SHUTTERSTOCK ©

Discover the Past at the National Museum of Ireland – Archaeology

Ireland's most important cultural institution. **p60**

VANDERWOLF IMAGES / SHUTTERSTOCK ©

See How They Make the Black Stuff at the Guinness Storehouse

The world's most famous beer. **p92**

Explore the Beautiful Campus of Trinity College

Ireland's most beautiful university campus. **p36**

GIMAS / SHUTTERSTOCK ©

Visit one of Dublin's Earliest Christian Sites at St Patrick's Cathedral

Ireland's capital cathedral. **p94**

SAHANDPHOTOGRAPHY / SHUTTERSTOCK ©

SALVADOR MANIQUIZ / SHUTTERSTOCK ©

Learn about Irish History at Kilmainham Gaol

A prison of historical importance. **p96**

Tour Dublin Castle, Former Centre of British Rule

Seat of English power for 700 years. **p40**

MARIANGELA CRUZ / SHUTTERSTOCK ©

Examine Artefacts at the Chester Beatty Library

Magnificent collection of relics. **p42**

BARRY MASON / ALAMY STOCK PHOTO ©

YVKKAA / SHUTTERSTOCK ©

Appreciate Modern Art at Hugh Lane Gallery

Dublin's best modern art gallery. **p112**

Marvel at the Striking Christ Church Cathedral

Dublin's most eye-catching cathedral. **p76**

RODRIGO GARRIDO / SHUTTERSTOCK ©

SALVADOR MANIQUIZ / SHUTTERSTOCK ©

Admire Masterpieces of Art at the National Gallery

Treasures of art. **p62**

Dining Out

The choice of restaurants in Dublin has never been better. Every cuisine and every trend – from doughnuts on the run to kale with absolutely everything – is catered for, as the city seeks to satisfy the discerning taste buds of its diners.

EQROY / SHUTTERSTOCK ©

Bookings

You'll need to reserve a table for most city-centre restaurants Thursday to Saturday, and all week for the trendy spots. Most restaurants oper-ate multiple sittings, which means 'Yes, you can have a table at 7pm, but we'll need it back by 9pm'. A recent trend is to adopt a no-reservations policy in favour of a get-on-the-list, get-in-line policy.

When to Eat

Breakfast Usually eaten before 9am, although hotels and B&Bs will serve until 11am Monday to Friday, and to noon at weekends. Many cafes serve an all-day breakfast.

Lunch Usually a sand-wich or a light meal between 12.30pm and 2pm. On weekends Dubliners have a big meal (called dinner) between 2pm and 4pm.

Tea No, not the drink, but the evening meal – also confus-ingly called dinner. A Dubliner's main daily meal, usually eaten around 6.30pm.

Best for Irish Cuisine

Chapter One Who knew Irish cuisine could taste this good? (p122)

Clanbrassil House This intimate bistro is a foodie magnet. (p105)

Legal Eagle The best Sun-day roast in town. (p120)

Winding Stair Classic Irish dishes given an elegant twist. (p122)

Mr Fox Exquisite modern Irish cuisine. (p122)

Best for a Fancy Meal

Chapter One The food is sublime, the atmosphere is wonderfully relaxed. (p122)

OLIVIER CIRENDINI / LONELY PLANET ©

Restaurant Patrick Guilbaud Perhaps the best restaurant in Ireland, where everything is just right. (pictured above; p71)

Greenhouse Michelin-starred and marvellous: Irish meets Scandinavian. (p51)

Mr Fox A cool new take on Irish classics, in a gorgeous Georgian setting. (p122)

Best Casual Bites

Fumbally Great warehouse space with filling sandwiches and good coffee. (p104)

Coke Lane Pizza Their pizza and a pint is a (delicious) bargain. (p104)

Assassination Custard Inventive small plates in a teeny cafe. (p104)

Oxmantown Great sandwiches and breakfasts. (p120)

Best Midrange Restaurants

Pi Pizza Probably the best pizza in the city, if not the country. (p50)

Clanbrassil House Family-style dining in a chic neighbourhood restaurant. (p105)

Banyi Japanese Dining The best Japanese food in town. (p84)

Fish Shop Exquisitely fresh seafood at this tiny restaurant. (p121)

Best for Afternoon Tea

Merrion Decadent petit fours with an artistic flair. (p65)

Shelbourne A timeless experience. (pictured left; p65)

Westbury Hotel Afternoon tea with a view of Grafton St. (01-679 1122; www.doylecollection.com; Grafton St)

Dublin On a Plate

The Irish Fry

In an age of green juices and smashed avo breakfasts, the Irish fried breakfast – or just the 'fry' – is a tasty and filling reminder of a more traditional time.

Sausages Pork sausages are the breakfast's most essential ingredient

Buttered Toast Brown or white, no one dares eat a fry without slices of richly buttered toast.

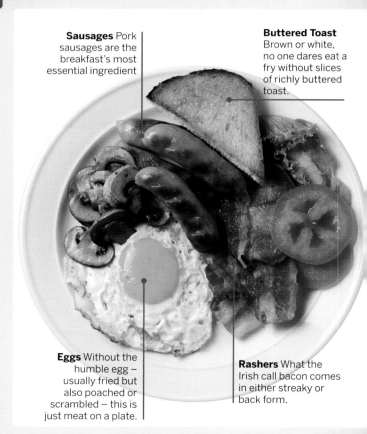

Eggs Without the humble egg – usually fried but also poached or scrambled – this is just meat on a plate.

Rashers What the Irish call bacon comes in either streaky or back form.

FREESKYLINE / GETTY IMAGES ©

★ Top Breakfasts

Sophie's @ the Dean (p51) There's perhaps no better setting in all of Dublin – a top-floor glasshouse restaurant with superb views of the city – to enjoy a fine breakfast.

Oxmantown (p120) Delicious breakfasts and excellent sandwiches make this cafe one of the standout places for daytime eating on the north side of the Liffey.

Farmer Brown's (p140) The hicky-chic decor and mismatched furniture won't be to everyone's liking, but there's no disagreement about the food, which makes this spot our choice for best brunch in Dublin.

Gerry's (p50) A no-nonsense, old-school 'caff' (the British Isles' equivalent of the greasy spoon) is rarer than hen's teeth in the city centre these days, which makes Gerry's something of a treasure.

The Classic Fry

Every hotel serves an Irish fry, but only the best ones (and nearly all B&Bs) will make them to order – otherwise you're stuck with the far inferior experience of picking ingredients out of metal containers at the buffet. An almost certain guarantee that it'll look (and taste) far stodgier than it should.

Oxmantown (p120)

DANITA DELMONT / ALAMY STOCK PHOTO ©

Bar Open

If there's one constant about life in Dublin, it's that Dubliners will always take a drink. Come hell or high water, the city's pubs will never be short of customers, and we suspect that exploring a variety of Dublin's legendary pubs and bars ranks pretty high on the list of reasons you're here.

The pub – or indeed anywhere people gather to have a drink and a chat – remains the heart of the city's social existence and the broadest window through which you can experience the essence of the city's culture, in all its myriad forms. There are pubs for every taste and sensibility, although the traditional haunts are about as rare as hen's teeth. But despair not, for it is not the spit or sawdust that makes a great Dublin pub but the patrons themselves, who provide a reassuring guarantee that Dublin's reputation as the pub capital of the world remains in perfectly safe hands.

Pub Etiquette

The rounds system – the simple custom where someone buys you a drink and you buy one back – is the bedrock of Irish pub culture. It's summed up in the Irish saying: 'It's impossible for two men to go to a pub for one drink'. Nothing will hasten your fall from social grace here like the failure to uphold this pub law. The Irish are extremely generous and one thing they can't abide is tight-fistedness.

Best Traditional Bars

John Mulligan's The gold standard of traditional. (p134)

The Long Hall Stylishly old-fashioned. (p52)

Stag's Head Popular with journalists and students. (pictured; p54)

Old Royal Oak A proper neighbourhood pub. (p105)

Best Musical Bars

O'Donoghue's The unofficial HQ of folk music. (p72)

Devitt's Trad music most nights. (p55)

DOMINIONART / SHUTTERSTOCK ©

Cobblestone Best sessions in town. (p122)

Auld Dubliner Traditional sessions for tourists. (p86)

Best New Bars

9 Below Super luxe bar for a fancy cocktail. (p53)

Fourth Corner A trendy spot on the edge of the Liberties. (p105)

Lucky Duck Modern vibes in a gorgeous old building. (www.theluckyduck.ie; 43 Aungier St)

Drop Dead Twice Rowdy and funky, with a BYO cocktail bar. (p105)

Best Club Nights

Grand Social Open, free jazz jam session on Monday. (www.thegrandsocial.ie; 35 Lower Liffey St)

Workman's Club Indie, house and disco in different rooms on Friday. (p87)

Mother Disco, electro and pop on Saturday...not for the faint-hearted. (p87)

Whelan's Electric acts on Thursday. (p55)

Best Local Haunts

Fallon's The Liberties' favourite bar. (p107)

Old Royal Oak Shh. Strictly for insiders. (p105)

John Kavanagh's A poorly kept secret. (p123)

Need to Know

Opening Hours

Last orders are at 11.30pm from Monday to Thursday, 12.30am on Friday and Saturday and 11pm on Sunday, with 30 minutes' drinking-up time each night. However, many central pubs have secured late licences to serve until 1.30am or even 2.30am (usually pubs that double as dance clubs).

Tipping

The American-style gratuity is not customary in bars. If there's table service, it's polite to give your server the coins in your change (up to €1).

Dublin in a Glass

A Pint of Guinness

Like the Japanese Tea Ceremony, pouring a pint of Guinness is part ritual, part theatre and part logic. It's a five-step process that every decent Dublin bartender will use to serve the perfect pint.

The Head Those nitrogen bubbles settle in a nice, creamy head.

The Top-Off Once settled, it's filled to the top so the head sits barely above the rim.

The First Pour A smooth pour should fill the glass to about three-quarters full.

The Bump The contour bump on the pint glass pushes the nitrogen bubbles into the centre of the pint.

VENGEROF / SHUTTERSTOCK ©

★ Top Pints

Kehoe's (p52) This beautiful Victorian bar is the very exemplar of a traditional Dublin pub.

Stag's Head (p54) Built in 1770, remodelled in 1895 and thankfully not changed a bit since then, this superb pub is so picturesque that it often appears in films.

John Mulligan's (p134) This brilliant old boozer is a cultural institution, established in 1782 and in this location since 1854.

Walsh's (p123) If the snug is free, a drink in Walshs is about as pure a traditional experience as you'll have in any pub in the city.

Grogan's Castle Lounge (p52) Grogan's is a city-centre institution and has long been a favourite haunt of Dublin's writers and painters, and others from the alternative bohemian set.

History of Guinness

The world's most famous beer is a type of porter, a dark, well-hopped ale that was popular with porters in 18th-century London. Arthur Guinness recognised the popularity of the brew and began making his own version in 1778 at the brewery he established two decades earlier on the banks of the Liffey.

Grogan's Castle Lounge (p52)

ANNEMARIE MCCARTHY / LONELY PLANET ©

Treasure Hunt

If it's made in Ireland – or pretty much anywhere else – you can find it in Dublin. Grafton St is home to a range of largely British-owned high-street chain stores; you'll find the best local boutiques in the surrounding streets. On the north side, pedestrianised Henry St has international chain stores, as well as Dublin's best department store, Arnott's.

ARNDALE/SHUTTERSTOCK ©

Traditional Irish Products

Traditional Irish products such as crystal and knitwear remain popular choices, and you can increasingly find innovative modern takes on the classics. But steer clear of the mass-produced junk whose joke value isn't worth the hassle of carting it home on the plane: trust us, there's no such thing as a genuine *shillelagh* (Irish fighting stick) for sale anywhere in town.

Fashion

There's a burgeoning vintage-shopping scene, with a number of shops in Temple Bar well worth a rummage, and well-curated stalls in the city's various markets, too.

At the other end of the fashion spectrum, you'll find all the knit and tweed you want at Avoca Handweavers (p55).

Markets

In recent years Dublin has gone gaga for markets, but the fluctuating rental crisis has seen many of them pushed from location to location, which means it can be hard to keep track of what's happening where. The best now happen in static businesses, such as at Lucky's (p106) or the George (p54).

Best for Guaranteed Irish

Avoca Handweavers Our favourite department store in the city has myriad homemade gift ideas. (pictured above; p55)

Irish Design Shop Wonderful handicrafts carefully sourced. (p55)

Barry Doyle Design Jewellers Exquisite hand-crafted jewellery with unique contemporary designs. (p57)

ANNEMARIE MCCARTHY / LONELY PLANET ©

Ulysses Rare Books For that priceless first edition or a beautiful, leather-bound copy of Joyce's Dubliners. (pictured above; p57)

Best for Fashion

Louis Copeland Fabulous suits made to measure, as well as ready-to-wear suits by international designers. (p57)

Costume Exclusive contracts with some of Europe's most innovative designers. (p57)

Scout Stylish, modern basics. (www.scoutdublin.com; 5 Smock Alley Ct, Essex St W; ◷10.30am-6pm Mon-Wed, Fri & Sat, to 6.30pm Thu, noon-5pm Sun)

Best for Jewellery

Chupi Beautiful jewellery inspired by the Irish landscape. (p55)

MoMuse Delicate and elegant gold jewellery. (www.momuse.ie; Powerscourt Townhouse, S William St; ◷10.30am-6.30pm Mon-Wed, Fri & Sat, to 7pm Thu, 1-5pm Sun)

Barry Doyle Design Jewellers Handmade jewellery exceptional in its beauty and simplicity. (p57)

Rhinestones Fine antique and quirky costume jewellery from the 1920s to 1970s. (18 St Andrew's St; ◷9.30am-6.30pm Mon-Wed, Fri & Sat, to 9pm Thu, noon-6pm Sun)

Duty-Free

Non-EU residents are entitled to claim VAT (value-added tax) on goods (except books, children's clothing or educational items) purchased in stores operating the Cashback or Taxback return programme. Fill in a voucher at your last point of exit from the EU to arrange refund of duty paid.

Show Time

Believe it or not, there is life beyond the pub. There are comedy clubs and classical concerts, recitals and readings, marionettes and music – lots of music. The other great Dublin treat is the theatre, where you can enjoy a light-hearted musical alongside the more serious stuff by Beckett, Yeats and O'Casey – not to mention a host of new talents.

DIRK HUDSON / SHUTTERSTOCK ©

Bookings

Theatre, comedy and classical concerts are usually booked directly through the venue. Otherwise you can buy through booking agencies such as **Ticketmaster** (☎0818 719 300; www. ticketmaster.ie; St Stephen's Green Shopping Centre; 🚇all city centre, 🚊St Stephen's Green), which sells tickets to every genre of big- and medium-sized show – but be aware that it levies a 12.5% service charge.

Best for Live Music

Cobblestone For traditional music. (p122)

3 Arena Big-name acts only. (www.3arena.ie)

Whelan's Singer-songwriter HQ. (p55)

Workman's Club Who's cool, right now. (p87)

Best for Theatre

Gate Theatre Wonderful old classic. (pictured; p124)

Project Arts Centre For interesting fringe plays. (p87)

Bord Gáis Energy Theatre The best indoor venue in town. (p135)

Abbey Theatre A hotbed of talent. (p124)

Best for High Culture

National Concert Hall Country's top orchestral hall. (p55)

Abbey Theatre Top names in Irish theatre. (p124)

Bloomsday Making sense of Ulysses. (p25)

Culture Night Art, architecture and heritage. (p25)

Museums & Galleries

RACHEL MCCASLIN / SHUTTERSTOCK ©

It's not surprising that Ireland's capital and biggest city by far should have the bulk of the best museums and galleries, but Dublin still operates an unexpected cultural surplus. You can uncover the city's – and the nation's – history, examine its most important artefacts and gaze upon art from prehistory to the modern day.

Best Collections

Hugh Lane Gallery, Dublin Impressive collection of modern and contemporary art. (p112)

National Gallery The best mix of classical European and Irish art in the coutry (p62)

National Museum of Ireland – Archaeology Home to the finest collection of Celtic art in the world (p60)

Irish Museum of Modern Art The best of Irish contemporary art (p102)

National Museum of Ireland – Decorative Arts & History Social and military history of Ireland told through clothing, jewellery and uniforms (p118)

Best Small Museums

Marsh's Library An 18th-century library virtually unchanged since it opened. (p102)

Chester Beatty Library Fabulous collection of books, scrolls and antique objets d'art from all over the world. (p42)

Little Museum of Dublin The story of the capital told through crowd-sourced obejcts. (p48)

14 Henrietta Street 200 years of history in one Georgian house. (p118)

Best Interactive Experiences

Guinness Storehouse You get to drink the product - at the source. (p92)

Jameson Distillery Bow Street Sample a snifter of the hard stuff after finding out how it's made. (pictured; p119)

EPIC The Irish Emigration Museum Use your 'passport' to uncover the story of emigration. (p131)

Irish Family History Centre Explore your Irish roots through interactive screens. (p131)

Architecture

MAYDAYS / GETTY IMAGES ©

Dublin's skyline is a clue to its age, with visible peaks of its architectural history dating back to the Middle Ages. The city is older still, but few traces of its Viking origins remain and you'll have to begin your explorations in the 12th century. Dublin's architectural apotheosis, however, came in the 18th century, during the Georgian era.

Best Georgian

Leinster House Richard Cassels' home for the Duke of Leinster inspired James Hoban's design for the White House. (p68)

Charlemont House Lord Charlemont's city digs – now home to the Hugh Lane Gallery, Dublin – was one of Dublin's finest Georgian homes. (p112)

14 Henrietta Street Beautifully restored Georgian home built for a viscount. (p118)

Four Courts The highest courts in the land are in a magnificent building designed by Thomas Cooley and James Gandon. (p115)

Custom House James Gandon announced his arrival in Ireland with this architectural stunner. (p132)

Bank of Ireland Edward Lovett Pearce's grand design once housed the Irish parliament. (p49)

Best Modern

Bord Gáis Energy Theatre (2010) Daniel Libeskind's architectural chops brought to bear for this 2100-capacity theatre. (pictured; p135)

Grand Canal Square (2007) Martha Schwartz's beautifully designed square fronting the threatre is the city's most beautiful modern space. (p132)

Samuel Beckett Bridge (2007) Santiago Calatrava's wishbone design is one of the Liffy's most eye-catching crossings. (p129)

Convention Centre (2011) Kevin Roche's design features a huge glass 'tube' set at a 45-degree angle in the building. (p133)

Worth a Trip

Fittingly, the grandest Georgian pile in the city is **Áras an Uachtaráin** (p109) - the president's house - a grand Palladian lodge built in the Phoenix Park in 1751 to house the British viceroy. Free tours of the house are run by the **Phoenix Park Visitor Centre** (http://phoenixpark.ie).

For Kids

MICHELLE O'KANE / GETTY IMAGES ©

Kid-friendly? You bet. Dublin loves the little 'uns, and will enthusiastically 'ooh' and 'aah' at the cuteness of your progeny. But alas such admiration hasn't fully translated into child services such as widespread and accessible baby-changing facilities.

Dublin's Parks

While it's always good to have a specific activity in mind, don't forget Dublin's parks – from St Stephen's Green (p48) to Merrion Square (p67), from Herbert Park (p139) to Phoenix Park (p109), the city has plenty of green spaces for the kids to run wild in.

Make a Splash

Kids of all ages will love **Viking Splash Tours** (01-707 6000; www.vikingsplash.com; St Stephen's Green N; adult/child €25/13; ⏰every 30-90min 10am-3pm; gall city centre, 🚊St Stephen's

Green), where you board an amphibious vehicle, put on a plastic Viking hat and roar at passers-by as you do a tour of the city before landing in the water at the Grand Canal basin.

Best for Kids

Ark Children's Cultural Centre Programs and inter-

active experiences aimed at kids three to 14. (p82)

Dublin Zoo One of Europe's better zoos, with lots of activities for kids (pictured; p109)

Dublinia Interactive exhibits designed to appeal to younger visitors. (p81)

National Leprechaun Museum Explore the hidden world of the fairy folk. (p119)

Family Tips

Transport Children under five travel free on all public transport.

Pubs Unaccompanied minors are not allowed in pubs; accompanied children can remain until 9pm (until 10pm from May to September).

Resources Parents with young children should check out www.everymum.ie and www.babygoes2.com.

Under the Radar

ANNEMARIE MCCARTHY / LONELY PLANET ©

Small and easily managed, Dublin's city centre is packed with enough excitement to distract and divert even the most ardent repeat visitor. But Dublin is forever on the move, alert to new trends and responsive to the pull of its own forces that have defined so much of the city's current identity.

Surburban Dining

A growing number of the city's most interesting chefs are decamping to the suburbs – mostly chasing more affordable rents. Grainne O'Keefe's **Mae** (www. maerestaurant.ie) in fashionable Ballsbridge; Gareth Smith's Michael's (p140) in affluent Mount Merrion; and trendy street food collective Eatyard (pictured; p125) in the north city suburb of Drumcondra are just some tasty examples.

Culture Night

Forget St Patrick's Day, which makes most Dubliners wince: the best night of the year is **Culture Night** (www.culturenight.ie; ☉Sep), when museums, historic houses, private parks and other sites of cultural significance throw open their doors to the public. There are lectures, demonstrations, concerts, tours and other fun cultural events. All free, all absolutely wonderful. It's one of the best ways to experience the city.

Minor Museums

Some of Dublin's most interesting museums are its least visited. Try Marsh's Library (p102) as an alternative to the Long Room in Trinity College, while 14 Henrietta Street (p118) is a Georgian townhouse that tells 200 years of Dublin history in one building.

Festivals & Events

DAVE PRIMOV / SHUTTERSTOCK ©

Dublin enjoys a good celebration - of food, theatre, music and, of course, St Patrick, even if this giant festival's religious connections are a little threadbare. Whenever you visit, however, there's always bound to be something on.

Best Festivals

Culture Night (www.culturenight.ie; ⊙Sep) One night extravaganza of talks, performance and events.

Dublin Fringe Festival (www.fringefest.com; ⊙Sep) Best of contemporary theatre.

St Patrick's Festival (www.stpatricksfestival.ie; ⊙mid-Mar; pictured) The city goes wild.

Dublin LGBTQ Pride (www.dublinpride.ie; ⊙mid-Jun) A 10-day celebration of the LGBTIQ+ community.

Forbidden Fruit (www.forbiddenfruit.ie; 1-/2-day ticket from €69.50/129; ⊙Jun) Excellent indie-music fest.

Taste of Dublin (https://dublin.tastefestivals.com; Iveagh Gardens; €17.50-30.50, VIP tickets €47.50-71.50; ⊙mid-Jun) A weekend of gourmet goodness.

Temple Bar Trad Festival (www.templebartrad.com; ⊙Jan; 🖵all city centre) One of the best parties of the year.

Best Pure Dublin

Bloomsday (www.jamesjoyce.ie; ⊙16 Jun) A day for Joycean devotees to enjoy.

All-Ireland Finals Climax of the hurling and football championships, on first and third Sundays of September, respectively.

Dublin City Liffey Swim (www.leinsteropensea.ie/liffey-swim; ⊙22 Jul) 500 lunatics swim in the Liffey.

Christmas Dip at the Forty Foot A jump into the icy waters by Sandycove on Christmas Day at 11am.

Ticket Booking

Book tickets well in advance for the bigger festivals like the Fringe and Forbidden Fruit; you'll need some kind of divine help to score tickets for the All-Ireland Finals, but it's not impossible!

Four Perfect Days

Day 1

Start with a stroll through Trinity College, visiting the **Old Library** (pictured; p37) and the Book of Kells before ambling up **Grafton St** to **St Stephen's Green** (p48). For more beautiful artefacts, drop into the **Chester Beatty Library** (p42).

Pick your heavyweight institution, or visit all three: the **National Museum of Ireland – Archaeology** (p60), if only for the Ardagh Chalice and Tara Brooch, the **National Gallery** (p62) – be sure to check out the Jack B Yeats room – and the **Museum of Natural History** (p67), which the kids will surely enjoy.

Temple Bar's nighttime options include a traditional-music session or just straight-up drinking at any of the district's many **pubs** (p85).

Day 2

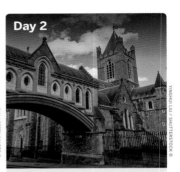

Begin with a little penance at Dublin's medieval cathedrals, **St Patrick's** (p94) and **Christ Church** (pictured; p76), before pursuing pleasure first at the **Teeling Distillery** (p102) and then at Dublin's most popular tourist attraction, the **Guinness Storehouse** (p92).

Go further west to Kilmainham, visiting first the fine collection at the **Irish Museum of Modern Art** (p102) before going out the back entrance and stepping into **Kilmainham Gaol** (p96), which offers an illuminating insight into Ireland's struggle for independence.

Walsh's (p123) of Stoneybatter is a superb traditional bar. Alternatively, you could take in a play at either the **Gate Theatre** (p124) or Ireland's national theatre, the **Abbey** (p124).

Day 3

ANDREW MONTGOMERY / LONELY PLANET ©

After walking the length of **O'Connell St**, explore the collection of the **Hugh Lane Gallery, Dublin** (p112). At **14 Henrietta Street** (p118) you'll discover the story of a Georgian townhouse; at **Jameson Distillery Bow Street** (p119) you can uncover the secrets of Irish whiskey.

The collection of the **National Museum of Ireland – Decorative Arts & History** (p118) is excellent. Further west is the **Phoenix Park** (pictured; p108), Europe's largest city park.

The biggest choice of nightlife is in the streets around **Grafton St** (p52): there are traditional pubs, trendy new bars and music venues.

Day 4

ANDREW MONTGOMERY / LONELY PLANET ©

The award-winning **Little Museum of Dublin** (p48) has a wonderful collection of local artefacts and mementos, including a lectern used by JFK and a room devoted to U2. From here, you can take an excellent **Green Mile** (p44) walking tour of St Stephen's Green.

Across the river, **EPIC The Irish Emigration Museum** (p131) is a multimedia exploration of the Irish diaspora, while nearby you can climb aboard the **Jeanie Johnston** (p132), a ship that carried some of those emigrants.

A visit to **O'Donoghue's** (p72), on Merrion Row, is guaranteed to be memorable. It's a beautiful traditional bar that's always full of revellers, and there's a good chance there'll be a trad-music session on (pictured).

Need to Know

For detailed information, see Survival Guide p145

Currency
Euro (€)

Language
English

Visas
Not required for citizens of Australia, New Zealand, the USA or Canada, or citizens of European nations that belong to the European Economic Area (EEA).

Money
ATMs are widespread. Credit cards (with PIN) are widely accepted in restaurants, hotels and shops.

Mobile Phones
All European and Australasian mobile phones work in Dublin, as do North American phones not locked to a local network. Prepaid SIM cards start from €20.

Time
Western European Time (UTC/GMT November to March; plus one hour April to October).

Daily Budget

Budget: Less than €150
Dorm bed: €16–28
Cheap meal in cafe or pub: €15–25
Bus ticket: up to €2.85
Some museums: free
Pint: €5.50–7

Midrange: €150–250
Budget hotel double: €100–150
Midrange hotel or townhouse double: €130–250
Lunch or dinner in midrange restaurant: €30–40
Guided tours and admission to paid attractions: €20

Top end: More than €250
Double in top-end hotel: from €250
Dinner in top-end restaurant: €60–120

Advance Planning

Two months before Book accommodation, especially for summer. Purchase tickets for major live gigs, especially big-name touring musicians and comedians.

Two weeks before Secure accommodation in low season. Book weekend performances for main theatres, and Friday or Saturday night reservations at top-end restaurants.

One week before Book weekend tables at the trendiest or most popular restaurants.

Arriving in Dublin

Most travellers will arrive in Dublin by air, but ferries from the UK arrive at the Dublin Port terminal.

✈ From Dublin Airport

Bus Public bus every 10 to 15 minutes to city centre between 6am and 12.30am.
Taxi Around 45 minutes to city centre, costing around €25.

⚓ From Dublin Port

Bus All buses (adult/child €3.50/2, 20 minutes) are timed to coincide with arrivals and departures.

Getting Around

ᚖ Bicycle

The city's rent-and-ride Dublin bikes scheme (three days, €5; www.dublinbikes.ie) is the ideal way to cover ground quickly. There are more than 100 stations throughout the city.

🚌 Bus

Buses run from around 6am to about 11.30pm. You'll need exact fare or a Leap Card (available from most newsagents).

🏍 Car & Motorcycle

Traffic in Dublin is a nightmare and parking is an expensive headache. Supervised and sheltered car parks cost around €4 per hour, with most offering a low-cost evening flat rate.

🚊 Tram

Most efficient way of getting around. The Green Line runs through O'Connell St and St Stephen's Green to Sandyford in south Dublin; the Red Line runs from the Point Village to Tallaght via the north quays and Heuston Station.

Dublin Neighbourhoods

North of the Liffey (p111)
Grittier than its more genteel southside counterpart, the area immediately north of the River Liffey offers a mix of 18th-century grandeur, traditional city life and the multicultural melting pot that is contemporary Dublin.

Temple Bar (p75)
Dublin's best-known district, where mayhem and merriment is standard fare. During daylight hours there are shops and galleries to discover.

Hugh Lane Gallery, Dublin

Dublin Castle

Christ Church Cathedral

Kilmainham Gaol

Guinness Storehouse

St Patrick's Cathedral

Chester Beatty Library

Kilmainham & the Liberties (p91)
Dublin's oldest neighbourhoods, immediately west of the south city centre, have a handful of big-ticket tourist attractions.

Grafton St & Around (p35)
Grafton St is both the city's most famous street and its unofficial centre, surrounded by a warren of side streets and alleys almost always full of people.

Docklands (p127)

The gleaming modern blocks of the Docklands – dubbed Silicon Docks – are home to digital tech giants. A couple of architectural beauties stand out among the modern buildings.

Merrion Square & Around (p59)

In exquisite Georgian architecture, here you'll find the perfect mix of imposing public buildings, museums, and private offices and residences.

The Southside (p137)

The neighbourhoods that border the southern bank of the Grand Canal are less about sights and more about the experience of affluent Dublin.

Trinity College

National Gallery

National Museum of Ireland – Archaeology

Explore
Dublin

Worth a Trip 🔭

City's Walking Tours 🥾

Ha'penny Bridge (p81) PAVEL L PHOTO AND VIDEO / GETTY IMAGES ©

Explore

Grafton St & Around

Busy, pedestrianised Grafton St is both the city's most famous street and its unofficial centre. You'll find the biggest range of pubs, shops and restaurants in the bustling hive that surrounds it, a warren of side streets and alleys that is almost always full of people.

The Short List

○ **Chester Beatty Library (p42)** *Exploring the collection of one of the finest museums in Ireland.*

○ **Old Library & Book of Kells (p37)** *Beholding a majestic library and the world's most famous illuminated gospel.*

○ **Little Museum of Dublin (p48)** *Examining the marvellous collection of donated historical objects.*

○ **A Night Out (p52)** *Dinner followed by a pint or more in a pub, such as Kehoe's.*

Getting There & Around

🚌 All cross-city buses make their way to – or through – this part of the city.

🚊 The Luas Green Line stops on the west side of St Stephen's Green.

🚶 Grafton St is in the heart of the city and no more than 500m from all other neighbourhoods (including the western edge of the Docklands).

Grafton St & Around Map on p46

Grafton St POPA IOANA MIRELA / SHUTTERSTOCK ©

Top Experience

Explore the Beautiful Campus of Trinity College

This calm and cordial retreat from the bustle of contemporary Dublin is Ireland's most prestigious university, a collection of elegant Georgian and Victorian buildings, cobbled squares and manicured lawns that is among the most delightful places to wander.

⊙ MAP P46, E1

☏ 01-896 1000

www.tcd.ie

College Green

admission free

🕑 8am-10pm

🚌 all city centre,

🚆 Westmoreland or Trinity

Old Library & Book of Kells

Trinity's greatest treasures are found within the **Old Library** (adult/student/family €11/11/28, fast-track €14/11/28; ⏰8.30am-5pm Mon-Sat, from 9.30am Sun May-Sep, 9.30am-5pm Mon-Sat, noon-4.30pm Sun Oct-Apr), built by Thomas Burgh between 1712 and 1732. The star of the show is the *Book of Kells*, a breathtaking, illuminated manuscript of the four Gospels of the New Testament, created around AD 800 by monks on the Scottish island of Iona, but more stunning still is the 65m Long Room, the library's main chamber, which houses around 200,000 of the library's oldest volumes.

Other displays include a rare copy of the **Proclamation of the Irish Republic**, read out by Pádraig Pearse at the beginning of the Easter Rising in 1916, as well as the so-called **harp of Brian Ború**, which was definitely not in use when the army of this early Irish hero defeated the Danes at the Battle of Clontarf in 1014. It does, however, date from around 1400, making it one of the oldest harps in Ireland.

Your entry ticket also includes admission to temporary exhibitions on display in the East Pavilion.

Front Square & Parliament Square

Through the elegant Regent House entrance are Front Sq and Parliament Sq, the latter dominated by the 30m-high **Campanile**, designed by Edward Lanyon and erected from 1852 to 1853 on what was believed to be the centre of the monastery that preceded the college. According to superstition, students who pass beneath it when the bells toll will fail their exams.

On your left is Richard Cassel's 18th-century **Dining Hall**; across from it is Sir William Chambers' Palladian **Examination Hall**, built in 1785.

★ Top Tips

o A great way to see the grounds is on a **walking tour** (Authenticity Tours; www.tcd.ie/visitors/tours; tours €6, incl Book of Kells €15; ⏰9.30am-3.40pm Mon-Sat, to 3.15pm Sun May-Sep, fewer midweek tours Oct & Feb-Apr), departing from the College Green entrance.

o Book a fast-track ticket online to get cheaper and speedier access to the *Book of Kells* and the Long Room.

✕ Take a Break

o Take your pick from a range of sweet and savoury crêpes at Lemon (p50), near the Nassau St entrance.

o Walk up Grafton St and head into Kehoe's (p52) for a pint.

History

The college was established by Elizabeth I in 1592 on land confiscated from an Augustinian priory in an effort to stop the brain drain of young Protestant Dubliners, who were skipping across to continental Europe for an education and becoming 'infected with popery'. Trinity went on to become one of Europe's most outstanding universities, producing a host of notable graduates – how about Jonathan Swift, Oscar Wilde and Samuel Beckett at the same alumni dinner?

Fellows' Square

West of the brutalist, brilliant **Berkeley Library** (Fellows' Sq; ⊘closed to public), designed by Paul Koralek in 1967, the **Arts & Social Science Building** (⊘closed to public) is home to the **Douglas Hyde Gallery of Modern Art** (www.douglashydegallery. com; admission free; ⊘11am-6pm Mon-Wed & Fri, to 7pm Thu, to 5.30pm Sat), one of the country's leading contemporary galleries. It hosts regularly rotating shows presenting the works of top-class Irish and international artists across a range of media.

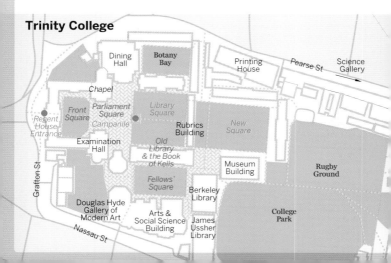

College Park

Towards the eastern end of the complex, College Park is a lovely place to lounge around on a sunny day and occasionally you'll catch a game of cricket, a bizarre sight in Ireland. Keep in mind that **Lincoln Place Gate** is located in the southeast corner of the grounds, providing a handy shortcut to Merrion Sq.

Science Gallery

Although it's part of the campus, you'll have to walk along Pearse St to get into Trinity's newest attraction, the **Science Gallery** (www. sciencegallery.ie; Naughton Gallery, Pearse St; admission free; ⊗exhibitions usually 11am-7pm Tue-Fri, to 6pm Sat & Sun). Since opening in 2008, it has proven immensely popular with everyone for its refreshingly lively and informative exploration of the relationship between science, art and the world we live in. Exhibits have touched on a range of fascinating topics including the science of desire and an exploration of the relationship between music and the human body.

A Catholic Ban

Trinity was exclusively Protestant until 1793, but even when the university relented and began to admit Catholics, the Catholic Church forbade it; until 1970 any Catholic who enrolled here could consider themselves excommunicated.

Top Experience 📷

Tour Dublin Castle, Former Centre of British Rule

If you're looking for a medieval castle straight out of central casting, you'll be disappointed; the stronghold of British power here for 700 years is principally an 18th-century creation that is more hotchpotch palace than turreted castle.

⊙ MAP P46, B2

www.dublincastle.ie

Dame St

guided tours adult/child €12/6, self-guided tours €8/4

🕘 9.45am-5.45pm, last admission 5.15pm

🚌 all city centre

Chapel Royal

As you walk into the grounds from the main Dame St entrance, there's a good example of extravagant 19th-century Irish architecture: on your left is the Victorian Chapel Royal (occasionally part of the Dublin Castle tours), decorated with more than 90 heads of various Irish personages and saints carved out of Tullamore limestone. The interior is wildly exuberant, with fan vaulting alongside quadripartite vaulting, wooden galleries, stained glass and lots of lively looking sculpted angels.

Upper Yard

The Upper Yard enclosure roughly corresponds with the dimensions of the original medieval castle. On your right is a Figure of Justice with her back turned to the city, reckoned by Dubliners to be an appropriate symbol for British justice. Next to it is the **Bedford Tower**, built in 1761 on the site of the original Norman gate. The Irish Crown Jewels were stolen from the tower in 1907 and never recovered.

Undercroft

The highlight of the guided tour is a visit to the **medieval undercroft** of the old castle, discovered by accident in 1986. It includes foundations built by the Vikings (whose long-lasting mortar was made of ox blood, eggshells and horsehair), the hand-polished exterior of the castle walls that prevented attackers from climbing them, the steps leading down to the moat and the trickle of the historic River Poddle, which once filled the moat on its way to join the Liffey.

The Rest of the Castle

Beside the Victorian Chapel Royal is the Norman **Record Tower**, the last intact medieval tower in Dublin. On your right is the Georgian **Treasury Building**, the oldest office block in Dublin, and behind you, yikes, is the uglier-than-sin **Revenue Commissioners Building** of 1960.

★ Top Tips

o The only way you'll get to see the castle's most interesting bits is by guided tour.

o The castle is occasionally used for government functions, so parts may be closed to the public.

✕ Take a Break

o Across the street from the main entrance is the Queen of Tarts (p84), a great spot for tea and cake.

o **Leo Burdock's** (www.leoburdock. com; 2 Werburgh St; cod & chips €10.25; ⏰11.30am-midnight Sun-Thu, to 1am Fri & Sat), around the corner, is Dublin's most famous fish-and-chip shop.

Grafton St & Around Tour Dublin Castle, Former Centre of British Rule

Top Experience 📸

Examine Artefacts at the Chester Beatty Library

The world-famous Chester Beatty Library, housed in the Clock Tower at the back of Dublin Castle, is not just Ireland's best small museum, but one of the best you'll find anywhere in Europe.
This extraordinary collection, so lovingly and expertly gathered by New York mining magnate Alfred Chester Beatty, is breathtakingly beautiful and virtually guaranteed to impress.

◎ MAP P46, A3

www.cbl.ie

admission free

🕙 10am-5pm Mon-Fri, from 11am Sat & Sun Mar-Oct, 10am-5pm Tue-Fri, from 11am Sat & Sun Nov-Feb

🚌 all city centre

Arts of the Book

The collection is spread over two levels. On the ground floor you'll find *Arts of the Book*, a compact but stunning collection of artworks from the Western, Islamic and East Asian worlds. Highlights include the finest collection of Chinese jade books in the world and illuminated European texts featuring exquisite calligraphy that stand up in comparison with the *Book of Kells*. Audiovisual displays explain the process of bookbinding, paper-making and printing.

Sacred Traditions

The 2nd floor is home to *Sacred Traditions*, a wonderful exploration of the world's major religions through decorative and religious art, enlightening text and a cool cultural-pastiche video at the entrance. The collection of Qu'rans dating from the ninth to the 19th centuries (the library has more than 270 of them; example pictured left) is considered by experts to be the best example of illuminated Islamic texts in the world. There are also outstanding examples of ancient papyri, including renowned Egyptian love poems from the 12th century, and some of the earliest illuminated gospels in the world, dating from around AD 200. The collection is rounded off with some exquisite scrolls and artwork from China, Japan, Tibet and Southeast Asia, including the two-volume Japanese *Chogonka Scroll*, painted in the 17th century by Kano Sansetu.

★ Top Tips

o There are free public tours of the museum on Wednesday at 1pm, Saturday at 2pm and Sunday at 3pm.

o The garden atop the building is a slice of serenity in the middle of the city.

o The museum hosts a series of free lunchtime talks; check the website for details.

✗ Take a Break

Lunch in the museum's **Silk Road Café** (www.silkroad kitchen.ie; mains €12) is a gourmet treat.

The excellent **Chez Max** (☏01-633 7215; www.chezmax.ie; 1 Palace St; mains €16-25; ☺noon-3.30pm & 5.30-10pm Mon-Thu, noon-3.30pm & 5.30-11pm Fri, noon-4pm & 5.30-11pm Sat, noon-4pm & 5.30-10pm Sun), by the main castle gate, is a fine French bistro.

Walking Tour 🥾

A Stroll Around St Stephen's Green

The most popular and best loved of the city's green spaces is St Stephen's Green, known simply as 'the green', where office workers roll up their sleeves to eat a sandwich beneath the sun at lunchtime, lovers steal a kiss on the grass and children feed clumps of bread to ever-appreciative ducks.

Walk Facts

Start Fusilier's Arch
End Huguenot Cemetery
Length 2.5km; 30 minutes

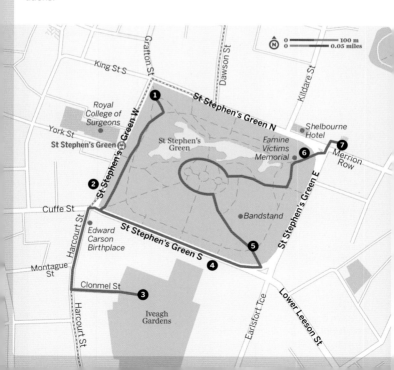

❶ Fusilier's Arch

The main entrance to St Stephen's Green is at the top of Grafton St, via the **Fusilier's Arch**, modelled to look like a smaller version of the Arch of Titus in Rome. The arch commemorates the 212 soldiers of the Royal Dublin Fusiliers who were killed fighting for the British in the Boer War (1899–1902).

❷ Unitarian Church

Walk down the western side of the green, past the stunning facade of the Royal College of Surgeons, the columns of which are still scarred by bullet holes from the 1916 Easter Rising. Just past it, on the same side, is the 1863 **Unitarian Church** (www.dublinunitarianchurch. org; admission free; ☉worship 7am-5pm), a favourite with Dubliners looking to marry in accordance with a range of personal beliefs.

❸ Iveagh Gardens

Cross onto Harcourt St, and walk past No 4, which was the birthplace of Sir Edward Carson, the founder of Northern Irish Unionism. Around the corner, off Clonmel St, is the little known but beautiful **Iveagh Gardens** (admission free), designed by Ninian Niven in 1863 as the private grounds of Iveagh House.

❹ Iveagh House

Walk back into St Stephen's Green and take a right along the park's southern edge. Across the street is **Iveagh House** (www.dfa.ie; ☉closed to public), two Georgian houses that were joined by Benjamin Guinness in 1862. Iveagh House was gifted to the state in 1939 and is now the Department of Foreign Affairs.

❺ The Three Fates

Just inside the southeastern entrance to the green is a fountain with a bronze **statue** in the middle, designed to represent the Three Fates. The work of artist Joseph Wackerle, it was a gift from the German people in 1956 for Ireland's role in securing foster homes for up to 500 refugee children after WWII.

❻ Tonehenge

Cut through the heart of the green, visiting the 1887 bandstand and the elegant flower beds before emerging at the northeastern corner. Just by the entrance is a memorial to the victims of the Famine, but it's dwarfed by the vertical slabs that encircle the statue of Wolfe Tone – hence, the whole thing is dubbed **'Tonehenge'**.

❼ The Beaux Walk

Across the street, heading towards Merrion Row, is the tiny **Huguenot Cemetery** (☉closed to public), established in 1693 by French Protestant refugees. All of the buildings here date from around the mid-18th century. The walk back towards Grafton St used to be called the Beaux Walk, and it's still full of fancy buildings (including the Shelbourne Hotel).

Grafton St & Around

A **B** **C** **D** **E** **F**

1 **2** **3** **4**

Parliament St

Lord Edward St

Dame St

Temple La S

Eustace St

Cope St

Anglesea St

Trinity St

College Green

Grafton St

Trinity College

College Park

Provost's Garden

Bank of Ireland

5

Irish Whiskey Museum 2

31

Suffolk St

Visit Dublin Centre

38

Wicklow St

Exchequer St

23

30

17

37

34

36

Dame Ct

Fade St

Great George's St S

24

8

18

Dame La

Palace St

Castle St

Dublin Castle

Hoey's Ct

Little Ship St

Great Ship St

Chester Beatty Library

Dublinlinn Garden

Chancery La

Golden La

Wood St

Great Longford St

Upper Stephen St

Great Stephen St

Aungier St

Bow La E

Lower Mercer St

Digges La

Lower Stephen St

22

15

Drury St

William St S

25

Chatham Row

Chatham St

Balfe St

Clarendon St

Westbury Mall

Coppinger Row

6

29

12

33

16

Anne St S

Lemon St

Duke St

9

35

32

20

Grafton St

King St S

St Stephen's Green Shopping Centre

Dawson St

Dawson

Molesworth St

Frederick St S

Setanta Pl

Nassau St

Kildare St

Schoolhouse La E

National Museum

Little Museum of Dublin

1

14

11

Grafton St & Around

Huguenot Cemetery

Merrion Row

Hume St

St Stephen's Green N

St Stephen's Green E

Lower Leeson St

Quinn's La

Leeson La

Earlsfort Tce

Lower Hatch St

St Stephen's Green

3

St Stephen's Green S

4 Museum of Literature Ireland

28

Iveagh Gardens

Upper Hatch St

St Stephen's Green W

Royal College of Surgeons

York St

Harcourt St

Clonmel St

Harcourt St

Cuffe La

Camden Pl

13

Peter Row

Bishop St

Upper Mercer St

Cuffe St

Montague St

7

Camden Row

26

Lower Kevin St

Wexford St

19

27

10

21

Lower Camden St

Peter St

New Bride St

Angier St

For reviews see	
◉ Top Experiences	p36
◉ Sights	p48
✖ Eating	p50
❄ Drinking	p52
● Entertainment	p55
▣ Shopping	p55

200 m

0.1 miles

N

5

6

7

8

A

B

C

D

E

F

5

6

7

8

Sights

Little Museum of Dublin

MUSEUM

1 ⊙ MAP P46, E4

This award-winning museum tells the story of Dublin over the last century via memorabilia, photographs and artefacts donated by the general public. The impressive collection, spread over the rooms of a handsome Georgian house, includes a lectern used by JFK on his 1963 visit to Ireland and an original copy of the fateful letter given to the Irish envoys to the treaty negotiations of 1921, whose contradictory instructions were at the heart of the split that resulted in the Civil War.

There's a whole room on the 2nd floor devoted to the history of U2, as well as the personal archive of Alfred 'Alfie' Byrne (1882–1956), mayor of Dublin a record 10 times and known as the 'Shaking Hand of Dublin'. Visit is by guided tour, which leaves on the hour, every hour. The museum also runs the Green Mile walking tour of St Stephen's Green (p44). (☑01-661 1000; www.littlemuseum.ie; 15 St Stephen's Green N; adult/student €10/8; ⊙9.30am-5pm, to 8pm Thu, last admission 7pm; ☐all city centre, ☐St Stephen's Green)

Irish Whiskey Museum

MUSEUM

2 ⊙ MAP P46, D1

If you'd like to learn a little more about one of Ireland's most famous tipples, spend an hour here. You'll find out why the Irish call it *uisce beatha* (water of life), how Dublin's whiskey trade collapsed and why it's on the rise again. The tour every half hour from 10.30am to 5.30pm also gives you a chance to taste at least three different types of whiskey. (☑01-525 0970; www.irishwhiskeymuseum.ie; 119 Grafton St; adult/child classic tours €20/€10, premium tours €23, blending experiences €30; ⊙10am-6pm; ☐all city centre)

St Stephen's Green

PARK

3 ⊙ MAP P46, E5

As you watch the assorted groups of friends, lovers and individuals splaying themselves across the nine elegantly landscaped hectares of Dublin's most popular green lung, St Stephen's Green, consider that those same hectares once formed a common for public whippings, burnings and hangings. These days, the harshest treatment you'll get is the warden chucking you out if you disturb the carefully tended flower beds. The buildings around the square date mainly from the mid-18th century, when the green was landscaped and became the centrepiece of Georgian Dublin. On the eastern side of the green is a children's playground and to the south there's a fine old bandstand, erected for Queen Victoria's jubilee in 1887. Musical performances often take place here in summer. Near the bandstand is a bust of James Joyce. (⊙dawn-dusk; ☐all city centre, ☐St Stephen's Green)

Museum of Literature Ireland

MUSEUM

4 ⊙ MAP P46, D6

Reopened in 2019, the Museum of Literature Ireland is a digital, interactive exploration of Ireland's deep literary heritage, from the Middle Ages to the present day. Highlights include Joyce's *Ulysses* notebooks as well as the very first print of the novel. The museum is in two stunning Georgian townhouses collectively known as Newman House, which in 1865 saw the establishment of the Catholic University of Ireland, the alma mater of Joyce, Pádraig Pearse and Eamon de Valera. (MoLI; ☎01-477 9810; www. moli.ie; 85-86 St Stephen's Green S; adult/child under 3yr/concession/ family €8/free/6/17, guided tour €12; ⏲10am-6pm; 🚍all city centre, 🚊St Stephen's Green)

Bank of Ireland

NOTABLE BUILDING

5 ⊙ MAP P46, D1

A sweeping Palladian pile occupying one side of College Green, this magnificent building was the Irish Parliament House until 1801 and was the first purpose-built parliament building in the world. The original building – the central colonnaded section that distinguishes the present-day structure – was designed by Sir Edward Lovett Pearce in 1729 and completed by James Gandon in 1733. (☎01-671 1488; College Green; ⏲10am-4pm Mon-Wed & Fri, to 5pm Thu; 🚍all city centre, 🚊Westmoreland)

St Stephen's Green

DERICK HUDSON / SHUTTERSTOCK ©

Grafton St & Around Sights

Eating

Pepper Pot
CAFE €

Everything is baked and made daily at the lovely cafe (see 33 🅐 Map p46, D2) on the 1st-floor balcony of the Powerscourt Townhouse (p56). The salads with homemade brown bread are delicious, but the real treat is the soup of the day (€6) – the ideal liquid lunch. (www.thepepperpot.ie; Powerscourt Townhouse, S William St; mains €6-10; ⊙10am-6pm Mon-Fri, from 9am Sat, noon-6pm Sun; 🚇 all city centre)

Lemon
CRÊPES €

6 ❌ MAP P46, C2

Dublin's best pancake joint serves a wide range of sweet and savoury crêpes – those paper-thin ones stuffed with a variety of goodies and smothered in toppings – along with super coffee in a buzzy atmosphere. (www.lemonco.com; 66 S William St; pancakes from €4.70; ⊙7.30am-7.30pm Mon-Wed & Fri, to 8.30pm Thu, 8.30am-7.30pm Sat, 9.40am-6.30pm Sun; 🛜; 🚇 all city centre)

Gerry's
CAFE €

7 ❌ MAP P46, C7

A no-nonsense, old-school 'caff' (the British Isles' equivalent of the greasy spoon) is rarer than hen's teeth in the city centre these days, which makes Gerry's something of a treasure. You won't find a more authentic spot to enjoy a traditional Irish fry-up. If you want healthy, it always does porridge, but what's the point? (6 Montague St; Irish fry-up €6.50; ⊙8am-2pm Mon-Fri, to 2.30pm Sat; 🚇 14, 15, 65, 83)

Pi Pizza
PIZZA €€

8 ❌ MAP P46, B2

Reg White cut his pie-making teeth at flour + water in San Francisco before opening this fabulous restaurant in 2018, and it's a contender for best pizzeria in town. The smallish menu has just eight pizzas, each an inspired interpretation of a Neapolitan classic. Highly recommended are the *funghi* (mushroom) or broccolini 'white' pizzas made without the tomato layer. (www.pipizzas.ie; 73-83 S Great George's St; pizzas €9-16; ⊙noon-10pm Sun-Wed, to 10.30pm Thu-Sat; 🚇 all city centre)

Featherblade
STEAK €€

9 ❌ MAP P46, E3

With an emphasis on more unusual cuts of beef — think *picanha* (sirloin cap) not fillet — this steakhouse offers amazing value for money. If you spot the West Cork Wagyu on the menu, snap it up — you couldn't ask for a more flavourful cut of beef. The wine menu is well priced too, with a number available on tap. (📞01-679 8814; www.featherblade.ie; 51B Dawson St; steaks €14-15; ⊙noon-3pm & 5-10.30pm Mon-Fri, noon-late Sat, 1-10pm Sun; 🚇 all city centre)

Hang Dai   CHINESE €€

10 🍴 MAP P46, B8

You'll need a reservation to get a seat at the bar or in one of the carriage booths of this super-trendy spot, designed to look like the inside of a railway carriage. The low red lighting and soulful tunes give off the ambience of a '70s porn theatre. The food, however – contemporary versions of Chinese classics – is excellent. (📞01-545 8888; www.hangdaichinese.com; 20 Lower Camden St; mains €17-29; ⏰5pm-midnight Tue-Sat, to 9.30pm Sun; 🚌14, 15, 65, 83)

Pig's Ear   MODERN IRISH €€

11 🍴 MAP P46, F3

Looking over the playing fields of Trinity College (p36) – which counts as a view in Dublin – this fashionably formal restaurant is spread over two floors and is renowned for its exquisite and innovative Irish cuisine, including dishes such as barbecued pork belly, short rib of Irish beef and a superb slow-cooked shepherd's pie. (📞01-670 3865; www.thepigsear. com; 4 Nassau St; mains €19-30; ⏰noon-2.45pm & 5.30-10pm Mon-Sat; 🚌all city centre)

Coppinger Row   MEDITERRANEAN €€

12 🍴 MAP P46, C3

Virtually all of the Mediterranean basin is represented on the ever-changing, imaginative menu here. Choices include the likes of pan-fried hake with mussels, baby potato and curried broth; or crispy pork belly with mustard mash, caramelised apple and black pudding. A nice touch are the filtered still and sparkling waters (€1): 50% goes to the Movember men's health charity. (📞01-672 9884; www. coppingerrow.com; Coppinger Row; mains €21-29; ⏰noon-11pm; 🚌all city centre)

Sophie's @ the Dean   ITALIAN €€

13 🍴 MAP P46, C7

There's perhaps no better setting in all of Dublin – a top-floor glasshouse restaurant with superb views of the city – in which to enjoy this quirky take on Italian cuisine. Delicious pizzas come with nontraditional toppings (smoked brisket with barbecue mustard?) and the 8oz fillet steak is done to perfection. A good spot for breakfast too. (📞01-607 8100; www.sophies.ie; 33 Harcourt St; mains €14-34; ⏰7am-10.30pm Mon-Wed, to 1.30am Thu-Fri, 8am-1.30am Sat, 8am-10.30pm Sun; 🚌10, 11, 13, 14, 15A, 🚇Harcourt)

Greenhouse   SCANDINAVIAN €€€

14 🍴 MAP P46, E4

Chef Mickael Viljanen might just be the one of the most exciting chefs working in Ireland today thanks to his Scandi-influenced tasting menus, which have made this arguably Dublin's best restaurant. The lunchtime set menu is one of the best bargains in town – a Michelin-starred meal for less than 50 bucks. Reservations necessary.

(📞01-676 7015; www.thegreenhouse restaurant.ie; Dawson St; 2-/3-course lunch menu €45/55, 4-/6-course dinner menu €110/129; ⏰noon-2pm & 6-9.30pm Tue-Sat; 🚇all city centre, 🚊St Stephen's Green)

Drinking

No Name Bar

BAR

15 🚇 MAP P46, C3

A low-key entrance next to the trendy French restaurant **L'Gueuleton** (www.lgueuleton.com) leads upstairs to one of the nicest bar spaces in town, consisting of three huge rooms in a restored Victorian townhouse plus a sizeable heated patio area for smokers. There's no sign or a name – folks just refer to it as the No Name Bar. (www.nonamebardublin.com; 3 Fade St; ⏰1.30-11.30pm Mon-Wed, to 1am Thu, 12.30pm-2.30am Fri & Sat, noon-11pm Sun; 🚇all city centre)

Kehoe's

PUB

16 🚇 MAP P46, D3

This classic bar is the very exemplar of a traditional Dublin pub. The beautiful Victorian bar, wonderful snug and side room have been popular with Dubliners and visitors for generations, so much so that the publican's living quarters upstairs have since been converted into an extension – simply by taking out the furniture and adding a bar. (9 S Anne St; ⏰11am-11.30pm Mon-Thu, to 12.30am Fri & Sat, 12.30-11pm Sun; 🚇all city centre)

Grogan's Castle Lounge

PUB

17 🚇 MAP P46, C3

Known simply as Grogan's (after the original owner), this is a city-centre institution. It has long been a favourite haunt of Dublin's writers and painters, as well as others from the alternative bohemian set, who enjoy a fine Guinness while they wait for that inevitable moment when they're discovered. (www.facebook.com/groganscastle lounge; 15 S William St; ⏰10.30am-11.30pm Mon-Thu, to 12.30am Fri & Sat, 12.30-11pm Sun; 🚇all city centre)

The Long Hall

PUB

18 🚇 MAP P46, B3

A Victorian classic that is one of the city's most beautiful and best-loved pubs. Check out the ornate carvings in the woodwork behind the bar and the elegant chandeliers. The bartenders are experts at their craft, a rare attribute in Dublin these days. (51 S Great George's St; ⏰noon-11.30pm Mon-Thu, to 12.30am Fri & Sat, 12.30-11pm Sun; 🚇all city centre)

Against the Grain

CRAFT BEER

19 🚇 MAP P46, B6

An excellent pub for the craft-beer fans, which is no surprise considering it's owned by the Galway Bay Brewery. There's a dizzying selection of ales and beers on tap, and the barkeeps are generous when it comes to offering tasters to help in your decision-making. Order some chicken wings for soakage if you plan on staying a while... (www.gal waybaybrewery.com/againstthegrain; 11 Wexford St; ⏰noon-midnight Mon-Thu, to 2am Fri & Sat, 12.30pm-midnight Sun; 🚇all city centre)

9 Below

BAR

20 🚇 MAP P46, D4

This lavish bar is tucked into a basement on St Stephen's Green, with weathered alcoves and cosy corners in which you can hide away with a cocktail. The whiskey menu is extensive, but keep an eye on what you're ordering – a glass of the most expensive blend, Midleton Pearl 30th Anniversary, will set you back an eye-watering

€1200. Booking recommended. (📞01-905 9990; www.9below.ie; 9 St Stephen's Green; ⏰5-11.30pm Tue-Thu, to 12.30am Fri & Sat; 🚇all city centre)

J. O'Connell

PUB

21 🚇 MAP P46, B8

Probably as close to a country boozer as you could find in the city, O'Connell's is the kind of place that draws in a solid crowd of locals and regulars. There is a good selection of beers on tap as well. (📞01-475 3704; 29 S Richmond St; ⏰4-11.30pm Mon-Thu, to 12.30am Fri & Sat, to 11pm Sun; 🚇14, 15, 44, 65, 140, 142 from city centre)

The Long Hall

P.Mac's BAR

22 MAP P46, B3

This Brooklyn-style bohemian hang-out is full of mismatched vintage furniture, American-style pint glasses and an alternative soundtrack veering towards the '90s. It also has 30-odd taps serving a huge variety of craft beers. (www.facebook.com/pmacspub; 30 Lower Stephen St; noon-midnight Sun-Thu, to 1am Fri & Sat; all city centre)

Farrier & Draper CLUB

This opulent bar in the 18th-century Powerscourt complex (see 33 Map p46, D2) combines Prohibition-era cool (staff in *Peaky Blinders* hats and sleeve garters) and Georgian decadence (high-vaulted ceilings, lots of paintings on the walls). Upstairs, in what was once Lady Powerscourt's private quarters, is a late-night bar and a club; downstairs is the beautiful Epic Bar; and in the basement is an Italian restaurant, La Cucina. (01-677 1220; www.farrieranddraper.ie; Powerscourt Townhouse, S William St; 4pm-midnight Mon-Wed, to 1am Thu, noon-3pm Fri & Sat, noon-midnight Sun; all city centre)

Stag's Head PUB

23 MAP P46, C2

The Stag's Head was built in 1770, remodelled in 1895 and thankfully not changed a bit since then. It's a superb pub: so picturesque that it often appears in films and was featured in a postage-stamp series on Irish bars. A bloody great pub, no doubt. (www.stagshead.ie; 1 Dame Ct; 10am-11pm Sun-Thu, to 1am Fri & Sat; all city centre)

The George GAY

24 MAP P46, B2

The purple mother of Dublin's gay bars is a long-standing institution, having lived through the years when it was the only place in town where the gay crowd could, well, be gay. Shirley's legendary Sunday-night bingo is as popular as ever, while Wednesday's Space N Veda is a terrific night of cabaret and drag. (www.thegeorge.ie; 89 S Great George's St; weekends after 10pm €5-10, other times free; 2pm-2.30am Mon-Fri, from 12.30pm Sat, 12.30pm-1am Sun; all city centre)

Clement & Pekoe CAFE

25 MAP P46, C3

Our favourite cafe in town is this contemporary version of an Edwardian tearoom. Walnut floors, art deco chandeliers and wall-to-wall displays of handsome tea jars are the perfect setting in which to enjoy the huge range of loose-leaf teas and carefully made coffees, along with a selection of cakes. (www.clementandpekoe.com; 50 S William St; 8am-7pm Mon-Fri, 9am-6.30pm Sat, 11am-6pm Sun; all city centre)

Entertainment

Whelan's
LIVE MUSIC

 26 MAP P46, B7

Perhaps the city's most beloved live-music venue is this midsized room attached to a traditional bar. This is the singer-songwriter's spiritual home: when they're done pouring out the contents of their hearts on stage, you can find them filling up in the bar along with their fans. (01-478 0766; www.whelanslive.com; 25 Wexford St; 16, 122 from city centre)

Devitt's
LIVE MUSIC

27 MAP P46, B7

Devitt's – aka the Cusack Stand – is one of the favourite places for the city's talented musicians to display their wares, with sessions as good as any you'll hear in the city centre. Highly recommended. (01-475 3414; www.devittspub.ie; 78 Lower Camden St; from 9pm Mon & Tue, 9.30pm Wed & Thu, 7.45pm Fri & Sat, 6.30pm Sun; 14, 15, 65, 83)

National Concert Hall
LIVE MUSIC

28 MAP P46, E8

Ireland's premier orchestral hall hosts a variety of concerts year-round, with an increasingly diverse roster of performances including author interviews and spoken-word events. (01-417 0000; www.nch.ie; Earlsfort Tce; all city centre)

Shopping

Chupi
JEWELLERY

29 MAP P46, C3

Exceptional modern jewellery inspired by the Irish landscape and worn by all the city's style fiends. The pretty shop also stocks Irish-designed clothing and accessories. (01-551 0352; www.chupi.com; Powerscourt Townhouse, S William St; 10am-6pm Mon-Wed, Fri & Sat, to 7pm Thu, noon-5pm Sun; all city centre)

Irish Design Shop
ARTS & CRAFTS

 30 MAP P46, C2

Beautiful, imaginatively crafted items – from jewellery to kitchenware – carefully curated by owners Clare Grennan and Laura Caffrey. If you're looking for a stylish Irish-made memento or gift, you'll surely find it here. (01-679 8871; www.irishdesignshop.com; 41 Drury St; 10am-6pm Mon-Sat, 1-5pm Sun; all city centre)

Avoca Handweavers
ARTS & CRAFTS

31 MAP P46, D2

Combining clothing, homewares, a basement food hall and an excellent top-floor **cafe** (mains €7-18; 9.30am-4.30pm Mon-Fri, to 5.30pm Sat, 10am-5pm Sun), Avoca promotes a stylish but homey brand of modern Irish life – and is one of the best places to find

Best Shopping

The most interesting shops in town are in the warren of streets between Grafton and South Great George's Sts; here you'll also find some of the best lunch deals.

an original present. Many of the garments are woven, knitted and naturally dyed at its Wicklow factory. There's a terrific kids' section. (☎01-677 4215; www.avoca.ie; 11-13 Suffolk St; ☉9.30am-6pm Mon-Wed & Sat, to 7pm Thu & Fri, 11am-6pm Sun; ⛺all city centre)

Sheridan's Cheesemongers   FOOD

32 🅰 MAP P46, E3

If heaven were a cheese shop, this would be it. Wooden shelves are laden with rounds of farmhouse cheeses, sourced from around the country by Kevin and Seamus Sheridan, who have almost single-handedly revived cheese-making in Ireland. (☎01-679 3143; www.sheridanscheesemongers.com; 11 S Anne St; ☉10am-6pm Mon-Fri, from 9.30am Sat; ⛺all city centre)

Powerscourt Townhouse   SHOPPING CENTRE

33 🅰 MAP P46, D2

This absolutely gorgeous and stylish centre is in a carefully refurbished Georgian townhouse,

built between 1741 and 1744. These days it's best known for its cafes and restaurants but it also does a top-end, selective trade in high fashion, art, exquisite handicrafts and other chi-chi sundries. (☎01-679 4144; www.powerscourtcentre.ie; 59 S William St; ☉10am-6pm Mon-Wed & Fri, to 8pm Thu, 9am-6pm Sat, noon-6pm Sun; ⛺all city centre)

Article   HOMEWARES

Beautiful tableware and decorative home accessories (see 33 🅰 Map p46, D2) all made by Irish designers. Ideal for unique, tasteful gifts that you won't find elsewhere. (☎01-679 9268; www.articledublin.com; 1st fl, Powerscourt Townhouse, S William St; ☉10.30am-6pm Mon-Wed, Fri & Sat, to 7pm Thu, 1-5pm Sun; ⛺all city centre)

George's Street Arcade   MARKET

34 🅰 MAP P46, C2

Dublin's best nonfood market is sheltered within an elegant Victorian Gothic arcade. Apart from shops and stalls selling new and old clothes, secondhand books, hats, posters, jewellery and records, there's a fortune teller, some gourmet nibbles, and a fish and chipper that does a roaring trade. (www.georgesstreetarcade.ie; btwn S Great George's & Drury Sts; ☉9am-6.30pm Mon-Wed, to 7pm Thu-Sat, noon-6pm Sun; ⛺all city centre)

Ulysses Rare Books

BOOKS

35 🔒 MAP P46, E3

Our favourite bookshop in the city stocks a rich and remarkable collection of Irish-interest books, with a particular emphasis on 20th-century literature and a large selection of first editions, including rare ones by the big guns: Joyce, Yeats, Beckett and Wilde. (📞01-671 8676; www.rarebooks.ie; 10 Duke St; ⏰9.30am-5.45pm Mon-Sat; 🚌all city centre)

Barry Doyle Design Jewellers

JEWELLERY

36 🔒 MAP P46, C3

Goldsmith Barry Doyle's upstairs shop is one of the best of its kind in Dublin. The handmade jewellery – using white gold, silver and gorgeous precious and semiprecious stones – is exceptional in its beauty and simplicity. Most of the pieces have Afro-Celtic influences. (📞01-671 2838; www.barrydoyledesign.com; 30 George's St Arcade; ⏰10am-6pm Mon-Sat; 🚌all city centre)

Costume

CLOTHING

37 🔒 MAP P46, C3

Costume is considered a genuine pacesetter by Dublin's fashionistas; it has exclusive contracts with innovative designers such as Vivetta, Isabel Marant, Cedric Charlier and Zadig & Voltaire. (📞01-679 5200; www.costumedublin. ie; 10 Castle Market; ⏰10am-6pm Mon-Wed, Fri & Sat, to 7pm Thu, 2-5pm Sun; 🚌all city centre)

Louis Copeland

CLOTHING

38 🔒 MAP P46, D2

Dublin's answer to the famed tailors of London's Savile Row, this shop makes fabulous suits to measure, and stocks plenty of ready-to-wear suits by international designers. There's another outlet at **39-41 Capel St**. (📞01-872 1600; www.louiscopeland.com; 18-19 Wicklow St; ⏰9am-6pm Mon-Wed, Fri & Sat, to 8pm Thu, noon-5pm Sun; 🚌all city centre)

Explore ◈
Merrion Square & Around

Georgian Dublin's apotheosis occurred in the exquisite architecture and elegant spaces of Merrion and Fitzwilliam Sqs. Here you'll find the perfect mix of imposing public buildings, museums and private offices and residences. It is around these parts that much of moneyed Dublin works and plays, amid the neoclassical beauties thrown up during Dublin's 18th-century prime.

The Short List

○ **National Gallery (p62)** *Perusing the collection at Ireland's pre-eminent art gallery.*

○ **Museum of Natural History (p67)** *Visiting this antiquated museum, which has changed little since it was opened in the middle of the 19th century.*

○ **National Museum of Ireland – Archaeology (p60)** *Uncovering the fascinating treasures of the most important repository of Irish culture.*

○ **O'Donoghue's (p71)** *Enjoying a night of music and beer in the very epitome of an Irish traditional pub.*

○ **Fine Dining (p70)** *Feasting on the superb cuisine offered by some of Dublin's very best restaurants.*

Getting There & Around

🚌 Most cross-city buses will get you here (or near enough).

🚋 The most convenient DART stop is Pearse St, with the station entrance on Westland Row.

🚶 Merrion Sq is less than 500m from St Stephen's Green (and Grafton St).

Merrion Square & Around Map on p66

Merrion Square (p67) FAITHIE / SHUTTERSTOCK ©

Top Experience 📷

Discover the Past at the National Museum of Ireland – Archaeology

This is the mother of all Irish museums and the country's foremost cultural institution. One of four branches, this is the most important, home to Europe's finest selection of Bronze and Iron Age gold artefacts, the most complete collection of medieval Celtic metalwork in the world, and fascinating prehistoric and Viking relics.

◉ **MAP P66, A3**

www.museum.ie

Kildare St

admission free

🕙10am-5pm Tue-Sat, from 1pm Sun

🚌all city centre

Treasury

The Treasury is the most famous part of the collection, and its centrepieces are Ireland's best-known crafted artefacts, the **Ardagh Chalice** and the **Tara Brooch**. The 12th-century Ardagh Chalice is made of gold, silver, bronze, brass, copper and lead; it measures 17.8cm in length and 24.2cm in diameter and, put simply, is the finest example of Celtic art ever found. The equally renowned Tara Brooch was crafted around AD 700, primarily in white bronze, but with traces of gold, silver, glass, copper, enamel and wire beading, and was used as a clasp for a cloak.

Ór – Ireland's Gold

Elsewhere in the Treasury is this exhibition featuring stunning jewellery and decorative objects created by Celtic artisans in the Bronze and Iron Ages. Among them are the **Broighter Hoard**, which includes a 1st-century-BC large gold collar, unsurpassed anywhere in Europe, and an extraordinarily delicate gold boat. There's also the wonderful **Loughnashade bronze war trumpet**, which also dates from the 1st century BC. It is 1.86m long and made of sheets of bronze, riveted together, with an intricately designed disc at the mouth.

Kingship & Sacrifice

One of the museum's biggest showstoppers is the collection of Iron Age 'bog bodies' – four figures in varying states of preservation dug out of the midland bogs. The bodies' various eerily preserved details – a distinctive tangle of hair, sinewy legs and fingers with fingernails intact – are memorable, but it's the accompanying detail that will make you pause: scholars now believe that all of these bodies were victims of the most horrendous ritualistic torture and sacrifice – the cost of being notable figures in the Celtic world.

★ **Top Tips**

o If you don't mind groups, the themed guided tours will help you wade through the myriad exhibits.

o If you want to avoid crowds, the best time to visit is weekday afternoons, when school groups have gone, and never during Irish school holidays.

✕ **Take a Break**

o Head to the museum's excellent cafe **Brambles** (mains around €11; ⏱10am-5pm Tue-Sat, 1-5pm Sun & Mon) for fresh salads, sandwiches and hot dishes.

o Go around the corner to the Shelbourne (p65) for afternoon tea or a drink in the Horseshoe Bar.

Top Experience 📷

Admire Masterpieces of Art at the National Gallery

A stunning Caravaggio and a room full of the work of Ireland's pre-eminent artist, Jack B Yeats, are just a couple of highlights from this fine collection. Its original assortment of 125 paintings has grown, mainly through bequests, to more than 13,000 artworks, including oils, watercolours, sketches, prints and sculptures.

◉ MAP P66, B2

www.nationalgallery.ie

Merrion Sq W

admission free

🕐 9.15am-5.30pm Tue-Wed, Fri & Sat, to 8.30pm Thu, 11am-5.30pm Sun-Mon

🚌 4, 7, 8, 39A, 46A from city centre

The Taking of Christ

The absolute star exhibit from a pupil of the European schools is Caravaggio's sublime *The Taking of Christ,* in which the troubled Italian genius attempts to light the scene figuratively and metaphorically (the artist himself is portrayed holding the lantern on the far right). Fra Angelico, Titian and Tintoretto are all in this neighbourhood.

Irish Art

There is an emphasis on Irish art, and among the works to look out for are William Orpen's *Sunlight,* Roderic O'Conor's *Reclining Nude* and *Young Breton Girl,* and Paul Henry's *The Potato Diggers.* But the highlight, and one you should definitely take time to explore, is the **Yeats Room**, devoted to and containing more than 30 paintings by Jack B Yeats, a uniquely Irish impressionist and arguably the country's greatest artist. Some of his finest moments are *The Liffey Swim, Men of Destiny* and *Above the Fair*.

The Vaughan Collection

One of the most popular exhibitions occurs only in January, when the gallery hosts its annual display of the Vaughan Collection, featuring watercolours by Joseph Mallord William Turner (1775–1851). The 35 works in the collection are best viewed at this time due to the particular quality of the winter light.

The French Collection

The French section contains Jules Breton's famous 19th-century work *The Gleaners,* along with works by Monet, Degas, Pissarro and Delacroix, while Spain chips in with an unusually scruffy *Still Life with Mandolin* by Picasso, as well as paintings by El Greco and Goya, and an early Velázquez.

★ **Top Tips**

○ The best time to visit the gallery is Thursday evening, when it's open late and there are fewer visitors.

○ There are family workshops for kids to try their hand at art throughout the year, usually on Saturdays; check the gallery website for details.

✕ **Take a Break**

○ Coburg Brasserie (p70) in the Conrad Hotel is great for a classy lunch.

○ Drop into Doheny & Nesbitt's (p73) for a post-gallery pint and a chat.

Walking Tour 🥾

A Georgian Block

Although Dublin is rightfully known as a Georgian city and many of its buildings were built between 1720 and 1814, the style cast such a tall shadow over Dublin design that for more than a century afterwards it was still being copied.

Walk Facts
Start Kildare St
End National Gallery
Length 1.7km; one hour

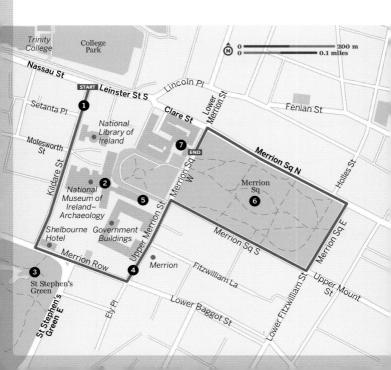

❶ Kildare St

Begin your amble at the northern end of **Kildare St**. This street is named after James Fitzgerald, the Duke of Leinster, who broke with 18th-century convention and moved to the then-unfashionable southside. 'Where I go,' he confidently (and correctly) predicted, 'society will follow.'

❷ Leinster House

Immediately after the Deane-designed **National Library of Ireland** (p69) is **Leinster House** (p68), the Palladian city pile that Fitzgerald commissioned Richard Cassels to build for him between 1745 and 1748. It is now the seat of both houses of the Irish parliament and inspired James Hoban's design for the White House.

❸ St Stephen's Green

The next building along the street is the **National Museum of Ireland – Archaeology** (p60), another Deane building, which opened in 1890 and has since been home to Ireland's most valuable cultural treasures. At the top of the street is **St Stephen's Green** (p48), the city's best-loved public square.

❹ Merrion Street

Turn left onto Merrion Row and walk along the green. You'll pass the historic **Shelbourne hotel** (www.theshelbourne.ie). Take another left onto **Merrion St**. On your right, No 24 in the row of elegant Georgian houses is the birthplace of Arthur Wellesley, the Duke of Wellington. It is now the very elegant hotel **Merrion** (www.merrion hotel.com).

❺ Museum of Natural History

On your left-hand side you'll pass the **Government Buildings** (p69), where the government of the day is based, and just past it, the rear entrance to Leinster House. The smaller building wedged in between the Government Buildings and Leinster House is the **Museum of Natural History** (p67), opened in 1857.

❻ Merrion Square

Further down on your right is **Merrion Square** (p67), the most elegant of Dublin's public spaces. The houses that surround it are magnificent: their doorways and peacock fanlights are the most photographed of the city's Georgian heritage and many of Dublin's most famous residents lived on it at one point or another.

❼ National Gallery

Walk around or through Merrion Sq, making your way back to West Merrion Sq and the **National Gallery** (p62), which opened in 1864. For the sake of symmetry, the facade is a copy of the Museum of Natural History facade.

E Hanover St

1

Pearse St

Trinity
College

College Park

**Pearse
Station**

Lower
Sandwith St

Lower
Pearse St

E Hanover St

Nassau St

2 Dawson

Leinster St

Lincoln Pl

Clare St

Westland Row

Cumberland St

Boyne St

Erne St Upper

Erne St Lower

Brunswick Pl

National
Library of
Ireland **7**

Kildare
St

Molesworth
St

**National
Gallery** **4**

**National
Museum of
Ireland –
Archaeology** **3**

Leinster
House
6

1
Museum of
Natural
History

Government **8**
Buildings

Oscar Wilde
Statue
5

Fenian St

Denzille La

Hogan
Pl

12 **17**

Holles St

Merrion Sq N

2
Merrion
Square

Merrion Sq S

Merrion Sq W

Merrion Sq E

Lower Mount St

Grattan St

**St Stephen's
Green N**

St Stephen's
Green

St Stephen's Green E

Merrion Row

Hume St

Ely Pl

14 **9** **11**

13 **18**

Fitzwilliam La

Lower Baggot St

3

Royal Hibernian
Academy (RHA)
Gallagher Gallery

Lower Fitzwilliam St

Upper Fitzwilliam St

Lower Pembroke St

Upper Pembroke St

15

Fitzwilliam Pl

Stephen's La

Upper Mount St

James's St E

James's Pl E

Lower Baggot St

Herbert St

Leeson La

Quinn's La

19

10

Lower Leeson St

Earlsfort Tce

Lower Hatch St

16

4
N
Fitzwilliam
Square

Pembroke Row

Lad La

Wilton Pl

Wilton Tce

Fitzwilliam Pl

Adelaide Rd

Grand Canal

Mespil Rd

6

Grand Pde

For reviews see

◉ Top Experiences p60
◎ Sights p67
✕ Eating p70
🍷 Drinking p71
✿ Entertainment p73

N 0 _____ 200 m
0 _____ 0.1 miles

Sights

Museum of Natural History

MUSEUM

1 🔘 MAP P66, B3

Affectionately known as the 'Dead Zoo', this dusty, weird and utterly compelling museum is a fine example of the scientific wonderment of the Victorian age. Its enormous collection of stuffed beasts and carefully annotated specimens has barely changed since Scottish explorer Dr David Livingstone opened it in 1857 – before disappearing into the African jungle for a meeting with Henry Stanley. It's temporarily closed for renovations, so look online to check its status. (www.museum. ie; Upper Merrion St; admission free; ⊙10am-5pm Tue-Sat, from 1pm Sun; 🚌7, 44 from city centre)

Merrion Square

PARK

2 🔘 MAP P66, C3

Merrion Sq is the most prestigious and, arguably, the most elegant of Dublin's Georgian squares. Its well-kept lawns and tended flower beds are flanked on three sides by gorgeous Georgian houses with colourful doors, peacock fanlights, ornate door knockers and, occasionally, foot-scrapers, used to remove mud from shoes. Over the last two centuries they've been used by some notable residents. (⊙dawn-dusk; 🚌all city centre)

Museum of Natural History

Royal Hibernian Academy (RHA) Gallagher Gallery

GALLERY

3 ◎ MAP P66, B4

This large, well-lit gallery at the end of a serene Georgian cul-de-sac has a grand name to fit its exalted reputation as one of the most prestigious exhibition spaces for modern and contemporary art in Ireland. Its exhibitions are usually of a very high quality, and well worth a visit. (☎01-661 2558; www.rhagallery.ie; 15 Ely Pl; admission free; ⏲11am-5pm Mon-Tue & Thu-Sat, to 8pm Wed, noon-5pm Sun; 🚌10, 11, 13B, 51X from city centre)

National Library of Ireland

DERICK HUDSON / SHUTTERSTOCK ©

Fitzwilliam Square

PARK

4 ◎ MAP P66, B5

The smallest of Dublin's great Georgian squares was completed in 1825. William Dargan (1799–1867), the railway pioneer and founder of the National Gallery, lived at No 2, and the artist Jack B Yeats (1871–1957) lived at No 18. In 2017 it began hosting a summer market of more than a dozen vendors. (⏲closed to public; 🚌10, 11, 13B, 46A from city centre)

Oscar Wilde Statue

STATUE

5 ◎ MAP P66, C2

Just inside the northwestern corner of Merrion Sq is a colourful statue of Oscar Wilde, who grew up across the street at No 1 (now used exclusively by the American University Dublin); Wilde wears his customary smoking jacket and reclines on a rock. Atop one of the plinths, daubed with witty one-liners and Wildean throw-aways, is a small green statue of Oscar's pregnant mother. (Merrion Sq; ⏲dawn-dusk; 🚌7, 8, 46A from city centre)

Leinster House

NOTABLE BUILDING

6 ◎ MAP P66, B3

All the big decisions are made at the Oireachtas (Parliament). This Palladian mansion was built as a city residence for James Fitzgerald, the Duke of Leinster and Earl of Kildare, by Richard Cassels between 1745 and 1748. Pre-arranged free **guided tours** (⏲10.30am,

Literary Addresses

Merrion Sq has long been the favoured address of Dublin's affluent intelligentsia. **Oscar Wilde** spent much of his youth at 1 North Merrion Sq, now the campus of the American College Dublin. Grumpy **WB Yeats** (1865–1939) lived at 52 East Merrion Sq and later, from 1922 to 1928, at 82 South Merrion Sq. **George (AE) Russell** (1867–1935), the self-described 'poet, mystic, painter and cooperator', worked at No 84. The great Liberator **Daniel O'Connell** (1775–1847) was a resident of No 58 in his later years. Austrian **Erwin Schrödinger** (1887–1961), he of the alive, dead or simultaneously both cat-paradox and co-winner of the 1933 Nobel Prize for Physics, lived at No 65 from 1940 to 1956. Dublin seems to attract writers of horror stories and **Joseph Sheridan Le Fanu** (1814–73), who penned the vampire classic *Carmilla,* was a resident of No 70.

11.30am, 2.30pm & 3.30pm Mon-Fri) are available when parliament is in session (but not sitting); entry tickets to the observation galleries are also available. (Oireachtas Éireann; ☎01-618 3271; www.oireachtas.ie; Kildare St; ☉observation galleries 2.30-8.30pm Tue, from 10.30am Wed, 10.30am-5.30pm Thu Nov-May; ◻all city centre)

National Library of Ireland
HISTORIC BUILDING

7 ◉ MAP P66, B2

The domed reading room of this august establishment is the main visitor highlight, and it was here that Stephen Dedalus expounded his views on Shakespeare in James Joyce's *Ulysses*. For everyone else, it's an important repository of early manuscripts, first editions and maps. It was built between 1884 and 1890 by Sir Thomas Newenham Deane to echo the de-

sign of the facade of the National Museum of Ireland – Archaeology. There's a **Genealogy Advisory Service** (☉9.30am-5pm Mon-Wed, to 4.45pm Thu & Fri) on the 2nd floor. (www.nli.ie; Kildare St; admission free; ☉9.30am-7.45pm Mon-Wed, to 4.45pm Thu & Fri, 9.30am-12.45pm Sat; ◻all city centre)

Government Buildings
NOTABLE BUILDING

8 ◉ MAP P66, B3

This gleaming Edwardian pile opened as the Royal College of Science in 1911 before being transformed into government offices in 1989. Free 40-minute tours include the office of the Taoiseach (Prime Minister), the Cabinet Room and the ceremonial staircase with a stunning stained-glass window, designed by Evie Hone (1894–1955) for the 1939 New York Trade Fair. Pick up tickets from 9.30am on the day of the tour at the Clare St entrance of the National Gallery. (www.taoiseach.gov.ie; Upper Merrion St; admission free; ☉tours hourly 10.30am-1.30pm Sat; 🚃7, 44 from city centre)

Eating

Etto

ITALIAN €€

 9 🚫 MAP P66, B4

Award-winning restaurant and wine bar that does contemporary versions of classic Italian cuisine. All the ingredients are fresh, the presentation is exquisite and the service is just right. Portions are small, but the food is so rich you won't leave hungry. The only downside is the relatively quick turnover; lingering over the excellent wine would be nice. Book ahead. (☏01-678 8872; www.etto. ie; 18 Merrion Row; mains €18-24; ☉noon-9.30pm Mon-Wed, to 10pm Thu-Fri, 12.30-10pm Sat; 🚃all city centre)

Coburg Brasserie

FRENCH €€

10 🚫 MAP P66, A5

The French-inspired, seafood-leaning cuisine at this revamped hotel brasserie puts the emphasis on shellfish: the all-day menu offers oysters, mussels and a range of 'casual' lobster dishes, from lobster rolls to lobster cocktail. The bouillabaisse is chock-full of sea flavours, and you can also get a crab-and-shrimp burger and an excellent yellowfin tuna Niçoise salad. Top-notch. (☏01-602 8900; www.thecoburgdublin.com; Conrad Dublin, Earlsfort Tce; mains €17-26; ☉6.30am-11pm; 🚃all city centre)

House

MEDITERRANEAN €€

This gorgeous bar (see 17 🔴 Map p66, A5) does a limited selection of main courses, but the real treats are the tapas-style sharing plates, which cover the full Mediterranean spread, from wild mushroom risotto and pulled pork to grilled halloumi and salt-and-pepper calamari. (☏01-905 9090; www. housedublin.ie; 27 Lower Leeson St; small plates €9-12, mains €15-26; ☉8am-midnight Mon-Wed, to 3am Thu & Fri, 4pm-3am Sat; 🚃11, 46, 118, 145 from city centre)

Ely Wine Bar

IRISH €€

11 🚫 MAP P66, B4

Scrummy organic burgers, nine-hour braised beef cheek and perfectly charred steaks are all on the menu in this basement restaurant. Meals are prepared with organic and free-range produce from the owner's family farm in County Clare, so you can rest assured of the quality. There's another **branch** (CHQ Bldg, ISFC, Georges Dock; 🚃George's Dock) in the Docklands. (☏01-676 8986; www.elywinebar.ie; 22 Ely Pl; mains €22-38; ☉noon-11.30pm Mon-Fri, 5pm-12.30am Sat; 🚃all city centre)

Musashi Hogan Place

JAPANESE €

12 ✖ MAP P66, D2

A branch of the expanding Musashi empire, serving the same excellent sushi, sashimi and maki as the original **restaurant** (15 Capel St; mains €12-17; ⏱noon-10pm; 🖵all city centre, 🚎Jervis) on the north side of the Liffey. (📞01-441 0106; www.musashidublin.com; 48 Hogan Pl; sushi €3-4, maki rolls €7-8, mains €14-15; ⏱noon-10pm Sun-Thu, to 11pm Fri & Sat; 🚎4, 7 from city centre)

Restaurant Patrick Guilbaud

FRENCH €€€

13 ✖ MAP P66, B4

Ireland's only two-Michelin star is understandably considered the best in the country by its devotees,

who proclaim Guillaume Lebrun's French haute cuisine the most exalted expression of the culinary arts. If you like formal dining, this is as good as it gets: the lunch menu is an absolute steal, at least in this stratosphere. Innovative and beautifully presented. (📞01-676 4192; www.restaurantpatrickguilbaud.ie; 21 Upper Merrion St; 2-/3-course set lunch €52/62, dinner menus €135-203; ⏱12.30-2.30pm & 7-10.30pm Tue-Fri, 1-2.30pm & 7-10.30pm Sat; 🚎7, 46 from city centre)

Drinking

O'Donoghue's

PUB

14 🍺 MAP P66, B4

The pub where traditional music stalwarts The Dubliners made their name in the 1960s still hosts

O'Donoghue's

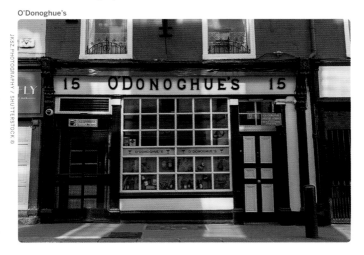

Merrion Square & Around Drinking

Five Books About Dublin

The Barrytown Trilogy (Roddy Doyle; 1992) Doyle's much-loved trilogy tells the story of the Northside working-class Rabbitte family. The three novels – *The Commitments* (1987), *The Snapper* (1990) and *The Van* (1991) – were published together in 1992.

Montpelier Parade (Karl Geary; 2017) The tale of the troubled relationship between the teenage Sonny and the much older Vera, set in the south Dublin neighbourhood of Monkstown, brings 1980s Dublin to life.

Dublin 4 (Maeve Binchy; 1982) Although written more than three decades ago, Binchy's examination of the tumult that afflicts a group of residents in Dublin's most affluent neighbourhood is just as poignant and relevant today.

Dubliners (James Joyce; 1914) Dublin serves as the unifying bedrock for this classic collection of 15 short stories that chronicle the travails of the capital and its middle-class residents at the turn of the 20th century.

Conversations with Friends (Sally Rooney; 2017) A brilliantly observed story of four characters – aspiring writer Frances, her ex Bobbi and older married couple Nick and Melissa – set against the backdrop of a post-economic-crash Dublin.

live music nightly, but the crowds would gather anyway – for the excellent pints and superb ambience, in the old bar or the covered coach yard next to it. (www.odonoghues. ie; 15 Merrion Row; ⏱10am-midnight Mon-Thu, to 1am Fri & Sat, 11am-midnight Sun; 🚌all city centre)

Toner's

PUB

15 🚊 MAP P66, B4

Toner's, with its stone floors and antique snugs, has changed little over the years and is the closest thing you'll get to a country pub in the heart of the city. Next door,

Toner's Yard is a comfortable outside space. The shelves and drawers are reminders that it once doubled as a grocery shop. (📞01-676 3090; www.tonerspub.ie; 139 Lower Baggot St; ⏱10.30am-11.30pm Mon-Thu, to 12.30am Fri & Sat, 11.30am-11.30pm Sun; 🚌7, 46 from city centre)

House

BAR

16 🚊 MAP P66, A5

Spread across two Georgian townhouses, this could be Dublin's most beautiful modern bar, with gorgeous wood-floored rooms, comfortable couches and even log fires in winter to amp up the cosiness. In the middle there's a lovely glassed-in outdoor space that on a nice day bathes the rest of the bar with natural light. There's also an excellent menu. (01-905 9090; www.housedublin.ie; 27 Lower Leeson St; 8am-midnight Mon, to 2am Tue & Wed, to 3am Thu & Fri, noon-3am Sat, noon-11pm Sun; 11, 46, 118, 145)

Square Ball   BAR

17 MAP P66, D2

This bar is many things to many people: craft beer and cocktail bar at the front, sports lounge and barbecue pit at the back and an awesome vintage arcade upstairs. There are also plenty of board games, so bring your competitive spirit. (01-662 4473; www.the-square-ball.com; 45 Hogan Pl; noon-11.30pm Tue-Thu, to 12.30am Fri & Sat, noon-11pm Sun; 4, 7 from city centre)

Doheny & Nesbitt's   PUB

18 MAP P66, B4

A standout, even in a city of wonderful pubs, Nesbitt's is equipped with antique snugs and is a favourite place for the high-powered gossip of politicians and journalists; Leinster House is only a short stroll away. (01-676 2945; www.dohenyandnesbitts.ie; 5 Lower Baggot St; 9am-12.30am Mon & Tue, to 1am Wed & Thu, to 2am Fri, 9.30am-2am Sat, 10.30am-midnight Sun; all city centre)

Entertainment

Sugar Club   LIVE MUSIC

19 MAP P66, A5

There are a huge variety of gigs, party nights and movie screenings in this intimate theatre-style venue on the corner of St Stephen's Green. (01-678 7188; www.thesugarclub.com; 8 Lower Leeson St; €7-20; 7pm-late; 7, 46 from city centre)

Explore

Temple Bar

Dublin's best-known district is the cobbled playpen of Temple Bar, where mayhem and merriment is standard fare, especially on summer weekends when the pubs are full and the party spills out onto the streets. During daylight hours there are shops and galleries to discover, which at least lends some truth to the area's much-mocked title of 'cultural quarter'.

The Short List

○ **Temple Bar Food Market (p83)** *Feasting on organic nibbles at Dublin's most exciting food market.*

○ **Claddagh Records (p88)** *Shopping for all kinds of Irish traditional and folk music in this wonderful record shop.*

○ **Christ Church Cathedral (p76)** *Visiting the most impressive-looking of Dublin's cathedrals.*

○ **Dublin Musical Pub Crawl (p81)** *Exploring the pubs of the area to a wonderful traditional soundtrack.*

○ **Gutter Bookshop (p87)** *Browsing the shelves of this locally owned bookshop.*

Getting There & Around

🚌 As Temple Bar is right in the heart of the city, all cross-city buses will deposit you by the cobbled, largely pedestrianised streets, making access – and escape – that bit easier.

🏃 Temple Bar is easily accessible on foot from Grafton St to the southeast, Kilmainham to the west and the north side of the river to the north.

Temple Bar Map on p80

The Temple Bar pub (p86) POPA IOANA MIRELA / SHUTTERSTOCK ©

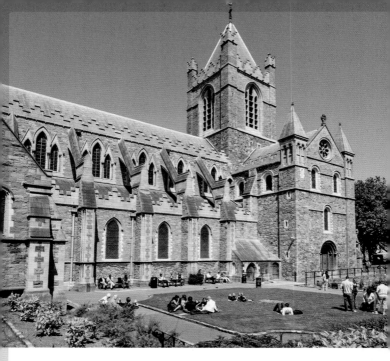

Top Experience 📸

Marvel at the Striking Christ Church Cathedral

Its hilltop location and eye-catching flying buttresses make this the most photogenic of Dublin's three cathedrals as well as one of the capital's most recognisable symbols.

◉ **MAP P80, A4**

www.christchurch
cathedral.ie

Christ Church Pl

adult/student/child
€7/5.50/2.50, with Dublinia €15/12.50/7.50

Chapter House & Northern Wall

From the southeastern entrance to the church-yard you walk past ruins of the chapter house, which dates from 1230. The main entrance to the cathedral is at the southwestern corner, and as you enter, you face the ancient northern wall. This survived the collapse of its southern counterpart but has also suffered from subsiding foundations (much of the church was built on a peat bog) and, from its eastern end, it leans visibly.

Strongbow Monument

The armoured figure on the tomb in the southern aisle is unlikely to be of Strongbow (it's more probably the Earl of Drogheda), but his internal organs may have been buried here. A popular legend relates an especially visceral version of the daddy-didn't-love-me tale: the half-figure beside the tomb is supposed to be Strongbow's son, who was cut in two by his loving father when his bravery in battle was suspect – an act that surely would have saved the kid a fortune in therapist's bills.

South Transept

The south transept contains the super baroque **tomb of the 19th Earl of Kildare**, who died in 1734. His grandson, Lord Edward Fitzgerald, was a member of the United Irishmen and died in the abortive 1798 Rising. The entrance to the **Chapel of St Laurence** is off the south transept and contains two effigies, one of them reputed to be of either Strongbow's wife or sister.

Crypt

Curiosities in the crypt include a glass display case housing a mummified cat in the act of chasing a mummified rat (aka Tom and Jerry), frozen midpursuit inside an organ pipe in the 1860s.

★ Top Tips

o The combination ticket that includes Dublinia is good value if you're visiting with kids.

o The cathedral has a weekly schedule of sung Masses, which can be very beautiful; check the website for details.

✕ Take a Break

o The Queen of Tarts (p84), with two locations around the corner from each other, does lovely cakes and coffee.

o Take your pick from Temple Bar's collection of pubs, but the Temple Bar (p86) is a classic.

★ Need to Know

⊙ 9.30am-5pm Mon-Sat, from 12.30pm Sun year-round, longer hours Mar-Oct

🚌 50, 50A, 56A from Aston Quay, 54, 54A from Burgh Quay

Walking Tour 🥾

Temple Bar's Secrets

Temple Bar is Dublin's main tourist hot spot, so it's often hard to find the more authentic experiences among its sea of plastic paddy tourism. But the cobbled streets do have plenty to offer in terms of retail and art, including lots of locally made, locally sourced items you can wear or eat.

Walk Facts

Start Crown Alley
End Old City
Duration 850m; 1 hour

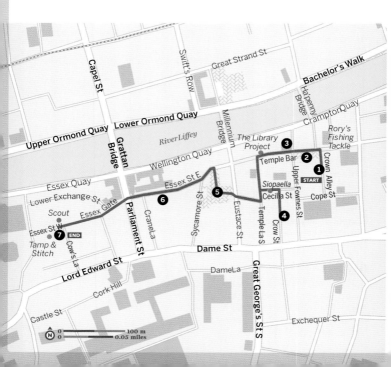

❶ Crown Alley

Just behind the Central Bank, Crown Alley stretches northward to Temple Bar Sq. Take a look at the huge art nouveau–style mural on the gable wall of Bloom's Hotel, featuring Leopold Bloom and Buck Mulligan from Joyce's *Ulysses*.

❷ Temple Bar Square

On weekends the square hosts a **book fair** (Temple Bar Sq; ⏱11am-5pm Sat & Sun; 🚆all city centre), and there's usually musical accompaniment, which gives a terrific atmosphere as people sit at the outdoor cafes and let the show unfold.

❸ Temple Bar

The street, rather than the neighbourhood, runs east–west along the square's northern edge. Peruse contemporary art in the **Temple Bar Gallery & Studios** (📞01-671 0073; www.templebargallery.com; 5 Temple Bar; admission free; ⏱11am-6pm Tue-Sat; 🚆all city centre) and check out photography from all over the world at the **Library Project** (http://tlp.photoireland.org; 4 Temple Bar; ⏱11am-6pm Tue-Fri, from noon Sat & Sun; 🚆all city centre).

❹ Crow Street

This is one of Temple Bar's genuinely alternative streets. On one side is All City Records one of the best in town for dance music. On the northwestern corner is part of the growing Siopaella empire.

❺ Meeting House Square

From Cecilia St, head west, through Curved St and down into Meeting House Sq, which on Saturdays is home to the Temple Bar Food Market, the best gourmet market in Dublin. On Sundays in summer, the square gives over to regular free concerts.

❻ Essex Street East

Walk west along Essex St, past Connolly Books , a bookshop with a leftist lean just below the New Theatre, which does all kinds of experimental theatre. Across the street is the Clarence Hotel, owned by U2, although it's been some years since any of the lads have been seen there.

❼ Old City

Cross Parliament St and you're now in Old City, named because the western end of Temple Bar is roughly where Viking Dublin was. Ironically, the area's newest, hippest boutiques are all here, including Scout and Tamp & Stitch. Take a load off and enjoy a nice coffee.

Temple Bar

F | E | D | C | B | A

1

2

3

4

Price's La

18

Icon
Factory

Aston Pl

1

Aston Quay

Bedford La

Fleet St

Bedford Row

14

Crampton Quay

Asdill's
Row

16

Ha'penny
Bridge

3

Temple Bar Sq

Crown Alley

22

11

Cope St

31 30

17

Upper Fownes St

32 15

Cecilia St

Crow St

21

29

Temple La S

Dublin
Musical
Pub Crawl

2

Foster Pl

Anglesea St

College Green

Bank of
Ireland

Suffolk St

Trinity St

St Andrew's St

Dame St

Dame La

Dame Ct

Great George's St S

Wicklow St

GRAFTON
STREET

Clarendon St

William St S

Drury St

George's St
Arcade

Exchequer St

Bachelor's Walk

Lower Ormond Quay

Quartier
Bloom

Swift's Row

Millennium
Bridge

Lower Fownes St

Temple Bar

Eustace St

9 7

5

6

27

Gallery of
Photography

Ark Children's
Cultural Centre

Palace St

Dublin Castle

Dublinn
Garden

National
Photographic
Archive

Wellington Quay

12 20 25

Essex St E

26

Crane La

River Liffey

Great Strand St

Capel St

Little Strand St

Upper Ormond
Quay

Grattan
Bridge

Parliament St

10 13

24

Cork Hill

Dublin
Castle

Castle St

Hoey's Ct

Werburgh St

Essex Quay

Lower Exchange St

Essex Gate

Essex St W

Fishamble St

Cow's La

28

23

33

Lord Edward St

Christ
Church
Cathedral

19

Christ Church
Guided Tours

8

Dublinia:
Experience Viking &
Medieval Dublin

4

Nicholas St

Winetavern St

Wood Quay

200 m
0.1 miles

N

For reviews see
◉ Top Experiences p76
◉ Sights   p81
◉ Eating   p83
◉ Drinking   p85
◉ Entertainment   p87
◉ Shopping   p87

Sights

Icon Factory
ARTS CENTRE

1 ⊙ MAP P80, F1

This artists' collective in the heart of Temple Bar hosts exhibitions on Ireland's cultural heritage. You'll find colourful, unique souvenirs celebrating the very best in Irish music and literature, and every sale goes towards the artists themselves. Take a stroll around their **Icon Walk** outside and get better acquainted with Irish playwrights, rock stars, sporting heroes and actors. (☏086 202 4533; www.iconfactorydublin.ie; 3 Aston Pl; admission free; ⊙11am-6pm; 🚌all city centre)

Dublin Musical Pub Crawl
WALKING

2 ⊙ MAP P80, F2

The story of Irish traditional music and its influence on contemporary styles is explained and demonstrated by two expert musicians in a number of Temple Bar pubs over 2½ hours. Tour groups meet upstairs in the **Oliver St John Gogarty** (www.gogartys.ie; 58-59 Fleet St; ⊙10.30am-2.30am Mon-Sat, noon-11.30pm Sun) pub. (☏01-475 8345; www.musicalpubcrawl.com; Anglesea St; adult/student €16/14; ⊙7.30pm daily Apr-Oct, 7.30pm Thu-Sat Nov-Mar; 🚌all city centre)

Ha'penny Bridge
BRIDGE

3 ⊙ MAP P80, E1

Dublin's most famous bridge is the Ha'penny Bridge, built in 1816. One of the world's oldest cast-iron bridges, it was built to replace the seven ferries that plied a busy route between the two banks of the river. Officially known as the Liffey Bridge, it gets its name from the ha'penny (half penny) toll that was charged until 1919 (for a time the toll was one-and-a-half pence, and so it was called the Penny Ha'penny Bridge). (🚌all city centre)

Dublinia: Experience Viking & Medieval Dublin
MUSEUM

4 ⊙ MAP P80, A4

A must for the kids, the old Synod Hall, added to Christ Church Cathedral (p76) during its late-19th-century restoration, is home to the seemingly perennial Dublinia, a lively and kitschy attempt to bring Viking and medieval Dublin to life. Models, streetscapes and somewhat old-fashioned interactive displays do a fairly decent job of it, at least for kids. (☏01-679 4611; www.dublinia.ie; Christ Church Pl; adult/student/child €10/9/6.50, with Christchurch Cathedral €15/12.50/7.50; ⊙10am-5.30pm Mar-Sep, to 4.30pm Oct-Feb; 🚌50, 50A, 56A from Aston Quay, 54, 54A from Burgh Quay)

Temple Bar Food Market

Gallery of Photography

GALLERY

5 ◉ MAP P80, D2

This small gallery devoted to the photograph is set in an airy three-level space overlooking Meeting House Sq. It features a constantly changing menu of local and international work, as well as photography classes. The downstairs shop is well stocked with all manner of photographic tomes and manuals. (www.galleryofphotography.ie; Meeting House Sq; admission free; ⊙11am-6pm Mon-Sat, 1-6pm Sun; 🚌all city centre)

Ark Children's Cultural Centre

ARTS CENTRE

6 ◉ MAP P80, D2

Aimed at youngsters between the ages of three and 14 years, the Ark runs a range of age-specific programs, talks and interactive experiences designed to stimulate participants' interest in science, the environment and the arts. The centre also has an open-air stage for summer events. (www.ark.ie; 11A Eustace St; 🚌all city centre)

National Photographic Archive

MUSEUM

7 ◉ MAP P80, D2

The archive of photographs taken from the mid-19th century onwards are part of the collection of the National Library, and so are open by appointment and only with a reader's ticket, which can be obtained from the main branch (p69). (www.nli.ie; Meeting House Sq; admission free; ⏰10am-1pm Tue-Thu, plus 2.30-4.30pm Wed; 🚌all city centre)

Christ Church Guided Tours

TOURS

8 🎯 MAP P80, A4

With its hilltop location and eye-catching flying buttresses, Christ Church Cathedral (p76) is the most photogenic of Dublin's cathedrals. Guided tours include the belfry, where you get to hear the campanologist explain the art of bell-ringing and have a go yourself. Under 12s are not allowed access to the belfry. (www.christchurch cathedral.ie; Christ Church Pl; tour €11; ⏰hourly 11am-noon & 2-4pm Mon-Fri, 2-4pm Sat; 🚌50, 50A, 56A from Aston Quay, 54, 54A from Burgh Quay)

Eating

Temple Bar Food Market

MARKET €

9 🍴 MAP P80, D2

Every Saturday this small square is taken over by food trucks, filling the air with the scent of pastries, artisan hot dogs, vegan curries and crêpes. The oyster bar is a highlight – grab half a dozen with a glass of chilled white wine and people-watch the afternoon away. (www.facebook.com/TempleBarFood

A Saucy Past

Purists may cry foul that Temple Bar never lived up to its cultural quarter moniker, but in many ways it's just staying true to its heritage. Imagine yourself back in 1742, for instance, when Handel was conducting the first-ever performance of his *Messiah* in **Fishamble St**, while just down the road on Bagnio Slip – now Lower Fownes St – gentlemen were lining up for an altogether different kind of distraction. Bagnio, from the Italian for bath house, had by then become the term for a brothel, and Temple Bar had plenty of them. It seems that pleasures of the flesh and of the mind have never been that far apart!

Market; Meeting House Sq; ⏰10am-5pm Sat; 🚌all city centre)

Sano Pizza

PIZZA €

10 🍴 MAP P80, C3

The authentic Neapolitan pizza served here is fantastic, with a chewy, charred crust and a sparse smattering of toppings. We love the Sapori del Sud, with spicy *nduja* (pork salami), fennel sausage, broccoli and mozzarella. And it's a bargain to boot. (☎01-445 3344; www.sano.pizza; 2 Upper Exchange St; pizzas €6-12; ⏰noon-10pm Sun-Wed, to 11pm Thu-Sat; 🚌all city centre)

Klaw

SEAFOOD €

11 🍴 MAP P80, E2

There's nothing sophisticated about this crab-shack-style place except the food: Irish oysters served naked, dressed or torched; Lambay Island crab claws served with a yuzu aioli; or half a lobster. Whatever you go for, it's all delicious; the 'shucknsuck' oyster happy hour is a terrific deal with all oysters costing €1.50. (www. klaw.ie; 5a Crown Alley; mains €8-15; ⏰noon-10pm Mon-Wed & Sun, to 11pm Thu-Sat; 🚇all city centre)

Bison Bar & BBQ

BARBECUE €

12 🍴 MAP P80, C2

Beer, whiskey sours and finger-lickingly good Texas-style barbecue – served with tasty sides such as slaw or mac 'n' cheese – is the fare at this boisterous restaurant. The cowboy theme is taken to the limit with the saddle chairs (yes, actual saddles); this is a place to eat, drink and be merry. (📞01-533 7561; www.bisonbar.ie; 11 Wellington Quay; mains €14-22; ⏰noon-9pm; 🚇all city centre)

Queen of Tarts

CAFE €

13 🍴 MAP P80, C3

This cute little cake shop does a fine line in tarts, meringues, crumbles, cookies and brownies, not to mention a decent breakfast: the smoked bacon and leek potato cakes with eggs and cherry tomatoes are excellent. There's another, bigger, branch around the corner on **Cow's Lane** (www. queenoftarts.ie; 3-4 Cow's Lane; mains €5-13; ⏰8am-7pm Mon-Fri, 9am-7pm Sat & Sun; 🚇all city centre). (📞01-670 7499; www.queenoftarts.ie; 4 Cork Hill; mains €5-13; ⏰8am-7pm Mon-Fri, from 9am Sat & Sun; 🚇all city centre)

Banyi Japanese Dining

JAPANESE €€

14 🍴 MAP P80, E1

This compact restaurant in the heart of Temple Bar has arguably the best Japanese cuisine in Dublin. The rolls are divine, and the sushi as good as any you'll eat at twice the price. If you don't fancy raw fish, the classic Japanese main courses are excellent, as are the lunchtime bento boxes. Dinner reservations are advised, particularly at weekends. (📞01-675 0669; www. banyijapanesedining.com; 3-4 Bedford Row; lunch bento €11, small/large sushi platter €19/32; ⏰noon-10.30pm; 🚇all city centre)

Seafood Cafe

SEAFOOD €€

15 🍴 MAP P80, E2

Sister restaurant to the seafood shack Klaw (p84), the Seafood Cafe is a more spacious outpost where you can enjoy native lobster dripping in garlic butter, roasted bone-in monkfish or Lambay Island crab with buttered sourdough toast. Delightful. (📞01-515 3717; www.facebook.com/klawcafe; 11 Sprangers Yard; mains €17-24; ⏰8am-9pm Mon-Thu, to 10pm Fri, 11am-10pm Sat, 11am-9pm Sun; 🚇all city centre)

Elephant & Castle

AMERICAN €€

16 ❌ MAP P80, E2

If it's massive New York–style sandwiches or sticky chicken wings you're after, this bustling upmarket diner – a long-time presence in Temple Bar – is just the joint. Be prepared to queue, though, especially at weekends when the place heaves with the hassled parents of wandering toddlers and 20-somethings looking for a carb cure for the night before. (📞01-679 3121; www. elephantandcastle.ie; 18 Temple Bar; mains €12-26; ⏰8am-11.30pm Mon-Fri, from 10.30am Sat & Sun; 🚌all city centre)

Drinking

Vintage Cocktail Club

BAR

17 🚌 MAP P80, E2

The atmosphere behind this inconspicuous, unlit doorway initialled with the letters 'VCC' is that of a Vegas rat pack hang-out or a '60s-style London members' club. It's so popular you'll probably need to book for one of the 2½-hour evening sittings, which is plenty of time to sample some of the excellent cocktails and finger food. (📞01-675 3547; www.vintagecocktailclub.com; Crown Alley; ⏰5pm-1.30am Mon-Fri, from 12.30pm Sat & Sun; 🚌all city centre)

Queen of Tarts

TYLER W. STIPP / SHUTTERSTOCK ©

Palace Bar PUB

18 MAP P80, F1

With its mirrors and wooden niches, the Palace (established in 1823) is one of Dublin's great 19th-century pubs, still stubbornly resisting any modernising influences from the last half-century or so. Literary figures Patrick Kavanagh and Flann O'Brien were once regulars and it was for a long time the unofficial head office of the *Irish Times*. (www.thepalacebardublin.com; 21 Fleet St; 10.30am-11.30pm Mon-Thu, to 12.30am Fri & Sat, 12.30-11.30pm Sun; all city centre)

Darkey Kelly's Bar & Restaurant IRISH PUB

19 MAP P80, B3

Once the home of Ireland's first female serial killer, Darkey's now boasts a killer whiskey selection instead. It has a decent range of craft beer, and is a compromise between the tourist bars of Temple Bar and more local boozers. The pint prices are on the steep side, but there's a great buzz and traditional music is guaranteed. (01-679 6500; www.darkeykellys.ie; 19 Fishamble St; 10.30am-11.30pm Mon-Thu, to 12.30am Fri & Sat, 12.30-11pm Sun; all city centre)

Liquor Rooms COCKTAIL BAR

20 MAP P80, C2

A subterranean cocktail bar decorated in the manner of a Prohibition-era speakeasy. There are lots of rooms – and room – for hip lounge cats to sprawl and imbibe both atmosphere and a well-made cocktail. There's dancing in the Boom Room, classy cocktails in the Blind Tiger Room and art deco elegance in the Mayflower Room. (087 339 3688; www.theliquorrooms.com; 5 Wellington Quay; 5pm-2am Sun-Tue, to 2.30am Wed, to 3am Thu-Sat; all city centre)

Temple Bar BAR

21 MAP P80, D2

The most photographed pub facade in Dublin, perhaps the world, the Temple Bar (aka Flannery's) is smack bang in the middle of the tourist precinct and is usually chock-a-block with visitors. It's good craic, though, and presses all the right buttons, with traditional musicians, a buzzy atmosphere and even a beer garden. (01-677 3807; www.thetemplebarpub.com; 48 Temple Bar; 10.30am-1.30am Mon-Wed, 10am-2.30am Thu-Sat, 11.30am-1am Sun; all city centre)

Auld Dubliner PUB

22 MAP P80, E2

Predominantly patronised by tourists, 'the Auld Foreigner', as locals have dubbed it, has a carefully manicured 'old world' charm that has been preserved – or refined – after a couple of renovations. It's a reliable place for a singsong and a laugh, as long as you don't mind taking 15 minutes to get to and from the jax (toilets). (01-677 0527; www.aulddubliner.ie; 24-25 Temple Bar; 10.30am-11.30pm Mon

& Tue, to 2.30am Wed-Sat, 12.30-11pm Sun; all city centre)

Entertainment

Smock Alley Theatre THEATRE

23 MAP P80, B2

One of the city's most diverse theatres is hidden in this beautifully restored 17th-century building. It boasts a broad program of events (expect anything from opera to murder mystery nights, puppet shows and Shakespeare) and many events also come with a dinner option. (01-677 0014; www.smockalley.com; 6-7 Exchange St; all city centre)

Mother CLUB

24 MAP P80, C3

The best club night in the city is ostensibly a gay night, but it does not discriminate: clubbers of every sexual orientation come for the sensational DJs – mostly local but occasionally brought in from abroad – who throw down a mixed bag of disco, modern synth-pop and other danceable styles. (www.motherclub.ie; Copper Alley, Exchange St; €10; 11pm-3.30am Sat; all city centre)

Workman's Club LIVE MUSIC

25 MAP P80, C2

A 300-capacity venue and bar in the former working-men's club of Dublin. The emphasis is on keeping away from the mainstream, which means everything from

singer-songwriters to electronic cabaret. When the live music at the Workman's Club is over, DJs take to the stage, playing rockabilly, hip-hop, indie, house and more. (01-670 6692; www.theworkmansclub.com; 10 Wellington Quay; free-€20; 5pm-3am; all city centre)

Project Arts Centre THEATRE

26 MAP P80, C2

The city's most interesting venue for challenging new work – be it drama, dance, live art or film. Three separate spaces allow for maximum versatility. You never know what to expect, which makes it all that more fun: we've seen some awful rubbish here, but we've also seen some of the best shows in town. (01-881 9613; www.projectartscentre.ie; 39 Essex St E; 45min before showtime; all city centre)

Irish Film Institute CINEMA

27 MAP P80, D3

The IFI has a couple of screens and shows classics and new arthouse films. The complex also has a bar, a cafe and a bookshop. (IFI; 01-679 5744; www.ifi.ie; 6 Eustace St; 11am-11pm; all city centre)

Shopping

Gutter Bookshop BOOKS

28 MAP P80, B3

Taking its name from Oscar Wilde's famous line from *Lady Windermere's Fan* – 'We are all in the

TAMUT / SHUTTERSTOCK ©

Lucy's Lounge

gutter, but some of us are looking at the stars' – this fabulous place is flying the flag for the downtrodden independent bookshop, stocking a mix of new novels, children's books, travel literature and other assorted titles. (☎01-679 9206; www.gutterbookshop.com; Cow's Lane; ☉10am-6.30pm Mon-Wed, Fri & Sat, to 7pm Thu, 11am-6pm Sun; ☐all city centre)

Claddagh Records   MUSIC

29 🔒 MAP P80, D2

An excellent collection of good-quality traditional and folk music is the mainstay at this centrally located record shop. The profoundly knowledgable staff should be able to locate even the most elusive recording for you. There's also a decent selection of world music. There's another **branch** (☎01-888 3600; 5 Westmoreland St; ☉10am-6pm Mon-Sat, from noon Sun) on Westmoreland St; you can also shop online. These outlets closed temporarily due to COVID-19, so check their current status online. (☎01-677 0262; www.claddaghrecords.com; 2 Cecilia St; ☉10am-6pm Mon-Sat, from noon Sun; ☐all city centre)

Jam Art Factory   DESIGN

30 🔒 MAP P80, E2

This quirky little shop is a good bet for souvenirs. It's crammed full of Irish art and design, so you can expect everything. Look for nostalgic gifts, hilarious comics or colourful renditions of the icons of the Dublin landscape. (☎01-616 5671; www.jamartfactory.com; 14 Crown Alley;

⊙11am-8pm Mon, from 10am Tue-Sat, 11am-8pm Sun; 🚇all city centre)

Lucy's Lounge VINTAGE

31 🏠 MAP P80, E2

Go through the upstairs boutique and you'll find a staircase to an Aladdin's basement of vintage goodies. You can easily while away an hour or two here before re-emerging triumphant with something unique to brighten up your wardrobe. Looking for something specific? The super-friendly staff know where everything is hiding. (📞01-677 4779; www.lucyslounge vintage.com; 11 Lower Fownes St; ⊙noon-6pm Thu-Sat, from 2pm Sun; 🚇all city centre)

Siopaella Design Exchange VINTAGE

32 🏠 MAP P80, E2

A secondhand shop like no other in Dublin, with rack upon rack of excellent vintage clothing. There's another branch on **Wicklow St**

(📞01-558 1389; 29 Wicklow St; ⊙10am-6pm Mon-Wed, to 7pm Thu-Sat, noon-6pm Sun; 🚇all city centre), which specialises more in designer pieces. (📞01-532 1477; www.siopa ella.com; 8A Crow St; ⊙noon-6pm Mon-Wed, Fri & Sat, to 7pm Thu; 🚇all city centre)

Cow's Lane Designer Mart MARKET

33 🏠 MAP P80, B3

On the steps of Cow's Lane, this hipster market brings together more than 60 of the best clothing, accessory and craft stalls in town. It's open from June to September; the rest of the year it moves indoors to **St Michael's and St John's Banquet Hall** (Oct-May), just around the corner.

Buy cutting-edge designer duds from the likes of Drunk Monk, punky T-shirts, retro handbags, costume jewellery by Kink Bijoux and even clubby babywear. (Cow's Lane; ⊙10am-5pm Sat Jun-Sep; 🚇all city centre)

Kilmainham & the Liberties

Dublin's oldest neighbourhoods, immediately west of the south city centre, have a handful of tourist big hitters, not least the Guinness Storehouse, Dublin's most-visited museum. Keeping watch over the ancient Liberties is St Patrick's Cathedral, the most important of Dublin's three cathedrals, while further west is a Victorian prison that played a central role in Irish history.

The Short List

○ **Kilmainham Gaol (p96)** *Taking a trip through Ireland's troubled history at this 18th-century prison.*

○ **Guinness Storehouse (p92)** *Sampling a pint at the factory where it all began in 1759.*

○ **Teeling Distillery (p102)** *Getting familiar with Irish whiskey at this newish distillery.*

○ **St Patrick's Cathedral (p94)** *Visiting Jonathan Swift's tomb in the cathedral where he served as dean for more than 30 years.*

○ **Irish Museum of Modern Art (p102)** *Admiring modern art in exquisite surroundings at a former hospital.*

Getting There & Around

🚌 Buses 50, 50A and 56A from Aston Quay and 55, 54A serve the cathedrals; 51, 51D, 51X, 69, 78 or 79 from Aston Quay for Kilmainham.

Kilmainham & the Liberties Map on p100

THE TASTING ROOMS

Top Experience 📷

See How They Make the Black Stuff at the Guinness Storehouse

More than any beer produced anywhere in the world, Guinness has transcended its own brand and is both the best-known symbol of the city and a substance with near spiritual qualities, according to its legions of devotees the world over. A visit to the factory museum where it's made is therefore something of a pilgrimage for many of its fans.

◎ MAP P100, E3

www.guinness-storehouse.com

St James's Gate, S Market St

adult/child from €18.50/16, Connoisseur Experience €55

🕐 9.30am-7pm Sep-Jun, 9am to 8pm Jul & Aug

The Museum

The most popular visit in town is this multi-media homage to Guinness in a converted grain storehouse that is part of the 26-hectare brewery. Across its seven floors you'll discover everything about Guinness and the history of the brewery. You'll even learn how to perfect the famous two-part pour.

The Original Lease

On the ground floor, a copy of Arthur Guinness' original lease lies embedded beneath a pane of glass in the floor. Wandering up through the various exhibits, including 70-odd years of advertising, you can't help feeling that the now wholly foreign-owned company has hijacked the mythology Dubliners attached to the drink, and it has all become more about marketing and manipulation than mingling and magic.

The Gravity Bar

Whatever reservations you may have about the marketing and hype of today's Guinness can be more than dispelled at the top of the building in the circular Gravity Bar, where you get a complimentary glass of Guinness. The views from the bar are superb, but the Guinness itself is as near-perfect as a beer can be.

The Connoisseur Experience

Aficionados can opt for the Connoisseur Experience, where you sample the four different kinds of Guinness – Draught, Original, Foreign Extra Stout and Black Lager – while hearing their story from your designated bartender.

Other Treats

Other add-ons include the STOUTie, the stout equivalent of latte art, where a pretty good likeness of yourself is drawn in the creamy head of the pint. Strictly for photographs, of course.

✗ Take a Break

○ In the shadow of the museum is the Legit Coffee Co (p104), which does good sandwiches and even better coffee.

○ For something a little stronger, Arthur's (p107) is a terrific little pub.

★ Getting Here

🚌 13, 21A, 40, 51B, 78, 78A, 123 from Fleet St,
🚊 James's

Kilmainham & the Liberties Guinness Storehouse

Top Experience 📷

Visit one of Dublin's Earliest Christian Sites at St Patrick's Cathedral

Situated on the very spot that St Paddy reputably rolled up his sleeves and dunked the heathen Irish into a well and thereby gave them a fair to middling shot at salvation, St Patrick's Cathedral is one of Dublin's earliest Christian sites and a most hallowed chunk of real estate.

◎ MAP P100, H3

www.stpatrickscathedral.ie

St Patrick's Close

adult/student €8/7

🕙 9.30am-5pm Mon-Fri, 9am-6pm Sat, 9-10.30am, 12.30-2.30pm & 4.30-6pm Sun Mar-Oct, reduced hours Nov-Feb

Swift's Tomb

Entering the cathedral from the southwestern porch you come almost immediately, on your right, to the tombs of Swift and his long-time companion Esther Johnson, aka Stella. On the wall nearby are Swift's own (self-praising) Latin epitaphs to the two of them, and a bust of Swift.

Boyle Monument

You can't miss the huge Boyle Monument, erected in 1632 by Richard Boyle, Earl of Cork. A figure in a niche at the bottom left of the monument is the earl's son Robert, the noted scientist who discovered Boyle's Law, which determined that the pressure and volume of a gas have an inverse relationship at a constant temperature.

St Patrick's Well

In the opposite corner, there is a cross on a stone slab that once marked the position of St Patrick's original well, where, according to legend, the patron saint of Ireland rolled up his sleeves and got to baptising the natives.

Door of Reconciliation

The door in the north transept has a hole in it through which in 1472 the earl of Kildare extended his hand as a peace offering to the earl of Ormond, who was on the other side – with a sword in his hand. Thankfully, the two earls made up and the expression 'to chance your arm' was born.

★ Top Tips

o Attend a sung Mass for the best atmosphere – at 11.15am on Sundays throughout the year, or at 9am Monday to Friday during school term only.

o Advance tickets are not valid on Sundays between 10.45am and 12.30pm and between 2.45pm and 4.30pm.

o Last admission is 30 minutes before closing time.

✕ Take a Break

o Cross Clanbrassil St and head for Fumbally (p104) for a sandwich or a hot bite.

o If you need something to fortify your spirits before or after your visit, Fallon's (p107) is one of Dublin's best pubs...and is conveniently only a short walk away.

★ Getting Here

🚌 50, 50A, 56A from Aston Quay, 54, 54A from Burgh Quay

Top Experience 📷

Learn about Irish History at Kilmainham Gaol

If you have any interest in Irish history, a visit to this infamous prison is essential. It was the stage for many of the most tragic and heroic episodes in Ireland's recent past, and its list of inmates reads like a who's who of Irish nationalism. Solid and sombre, its walls absorbed the hardship of British occupation and recount it in whispers to visitors.

◉ MAP P100, A3

www.kilmainhamgaol
museum.ie

Inchicore Rd

adult/child €9/5

🕑9am-7pm Jun-Aug,
9.30am-5.30pm Oct-Mar,
9am-6pm Apr, May & Sep

Guided Tour

Visits are by guided tour and start with a stirring audiovisual introduction, screened in the chapel where 1916 leader Joseph Plunkett was wed to his beloved just hours before his execution. The thought-provoking (but too crowded) tour takes you through the old and new wings of the prison, where you can see former cells of famous inmates, read graffiti on the walls and immerse yourself in the atmosphere of the execution yards.

Stone-Breakers' Yard

Fourteen of the rebel commanders were executed in the Stone Breakers' Yard, including James Connolly, who was so badly injured at the time of his execution that he was strapped to a chair at the opposite end of the yard, just inside the gate. The places where they were shot are marked by two simple black crosses. The executions set a previously apathetic nation on a course towards violent rebellion.

Asgard & Museum

Incongruously sitting outside in the yard is the *Asgard,* the ship that successfully ran the British blockade to deliver arms to nationalist forces in 1914. It belonged to, and was skippered by, Erskine Childers, father of the future president of Ireland. He was executed by Michael Collins' Free State army in 1922 for carrying a revolver, which had been a gift from Collins himself. There is also an outstanding museum dedicated to Irish nationalism and prison life.

★ **Top Tips**

• Arrive early to avoid the usually long queues; try to get on the first tour of the day (tours can't be booked in advance).

✖ **Take a Break**

• The Old Royal Oak (p105) is one of the city's most authentic traditional bars.

• For excellent contemporary Irish cuisine try **Union8** (☏ 01-677 8707; www.union8.ie; 740 S Circular Rd; mains €19-28; ⊙ 10am-3pm & 5-9.30pm Mon-Wed, to 9.30pm Thu-Fri, 10.30am-3.30pm & 5-9.30pm Sat, 10.30am-3.30pm & 5-8pm Sun).

★ **Getting Here**

🚌 69, 79 from Aston Quay, 13, 40 from O'Connell St

Walking Tour 🥾

Viking & Medieval Dublin

If you build a city out of wood and mud, it stands little chance of surviving through the ages. So it was with the original Viking settlement of Dyfflin, but if you look closely you'll see some traces of the city's Norse past. The medieval city has fared much better, mostly because stone was the primary building block.

Walk Facts

Start Essex Gate, Parliament St

End Dublin Castle

Length 2.5km; two hours

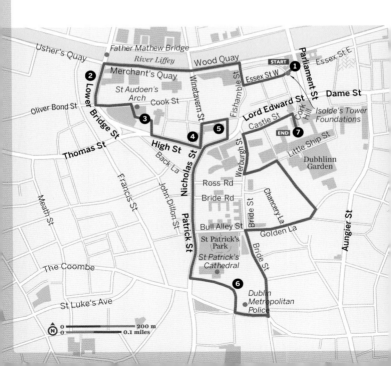

❶ Essex Gate

Once a main gate to the city, the only sign of **Essex Gate** is a bronze plaque on a pillar marks the spot where it stood. Further along, you can see the original foundations of the 13th-century **Isolde's Tower**, once part of the city walls, through a grill in the pavement.

❷ Brazen Head

Head north down to the river and proceed west along Merchant Quay. Opposite Father Mathew Bridge (built in 1818 on the spot that gave the city its Irish name, Baile Átha Cliath, or Town of the Hurdle Ford) is Dublin's oldest pub, the **Brazen Head** (☎01-679 5186; www.brazenhead.com; 20 Lower Bridge St; ☺10.30am-midnight Mon-Thu, to 12.30am Fri & Sat, 12.30pm-midnight Sun; ☐51B, 78A, 123 from city centre), dating from 1198 (the present building dates from a positively youthful 1668).

❸ St Audoen's Church

Take the next left onto Cook St to examine **St Audoen's Arch** (1240), the only remaining medieval gate of the 32 that were built. Climb up to the ramparts to the city's oldest existing churches, **St Audoen's Church of Ireland** (p103), built in 1190, and shouldn't be confused with the newer Catholic church next door.

❹ Dublinia

Leave the little park, join High St and head east until you reach the first corner. Here on your left is the former Synod Hall, now **Dublinia** (p81), where medieval Dublin has been interactively recreated.

❺ The Two Cathedrals

Next to Dublinia, Christ Church Cathedral was the most important medieval church *inside* the city walls; about 300m south along Nicholas St (which becomes Patrick St) stands the most important church outside the city walls, **St Patrick's** (p94).

❻ Marsh's Library

Along St Patrick's Close, beyond the bend on the left, is the stunningly beautiful **Marsh's Library** (p102), named after Archbishop Narcissus Marsh, dean of St Patrick's. Further along again on your left is the **Dublin Metropolitan Police building**, once the Episcopal Palace of St Sepulchre.

❼ Dublin Castle

Finally, follow our route up Bride St, Golden Lane and Great Ship St, and finish up with a long wander around **Dublin Castle** (p40), the centre of English and British rule in Ireland from 1204 to 1922.

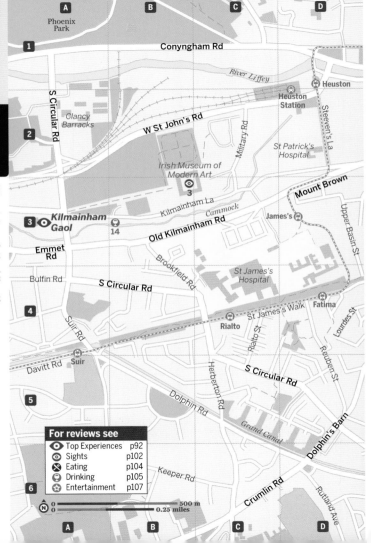

A Phoenix Park

B

C

D

1

Conyngham Rd

River Liffey

Heuston

Heuston Station

S Circular Rd

Clancy Barracks

W St John's Rd

2

Military Rd

St Patrick's Hospital

Steeven's La

Irish Museum of Modern Art
3

Mount Brown

Kilmainham La

Cammock

3 Kilmainham Gaol

14

Old Kilmainham Rd

James's

Upper Basin St

Emmet Rd

Brookfield Rd

St James's Hospital

Bulfin Rd

S Circular Rd

4

St James's Walk

Fatima

Lourdes St

Rialto

Rialto St

Reuben St

Suir Rd

S Circular Rd

Davitt Rd

Suir

Herberton Rd

Dolphin's Barn

5

Dolphin Rd

Grand Canal

Keeper Rd

Crumlin Rd

Rutland Ave

6

For reviews see	
◉ Top Experiences	p92
◉ Sights	p102
✕ Eating	p104
⬤ Drinking	p105
★ Entertainment	p107

N 0 _____ 500 m
   0 _____ 0.25 miles

E

Museum

Wolfe Tone Quay

F

Blackhall Pl

Benburb St

Queen St

Smithfield

Bow St

Ellis Quay

James Joyce Bridge

Smithfield

G

Lower Church St

Mary's La

Four Courts

H

Capel St

Arran St E

1

Arran Quay

Usher's Quay

Four Courts

Upper Ormond Quay

Essex Quay

Watling St

Bridgefoot St

St Augustine St

St Audoen's Church of Ireland

6

Winetavern St

2

Pearse Lyons Distillery

4 Roe & Co
Distillery

Oliver Bond St

Lower Bridge St

High St

5 James's St

18

19

Guinness Storehouse

Rainsford St

Thomas St

21 13

15

High St

Nicholas St

St Patrick's Cathedral

Bride St

3

9

Bellevue

Robert St

Marrowbone La

Earl St S

17

Meath St

10

Meath Pl

Catherine St

Swift's Al

Francis St

16 1

Marsh's Library

Long's Pl

Pimlico

John St S

Ardee St

Carman's Hall

The Coombe

Dublin Liberties Distillery

20

Upper Kevin St

New St

8

New Bride St

4

Cork St

Newmarket

Teeling Distillery

2

7

Mill St

New Row S

11

Long La

Dolphin's Barn

Fingal St

Brown St S

St Thomas Rd

O'Curry Rd

Clarence Mangan Rd

Blackpitts

Lower Clanbrassil St

St Teresa's Gardens

Donore Ave

Susan Tce

Dufferin Ave

Ingram Rd

DOLPHIN'S BARN

12

Emorville Ave

Arnott St

Emor St

5

S Circular Rd

S Circular Rd

Upper Clanbrassil St

Longwood Ave

Portobello Rd

6

Parnell Rd

Grove Rd

E

F

G

H

Sights

Marsh's Library
LIBRARY

1 ⊙ MAP P100, H3

This magnificently preserved scholars' library, virtually unchanged in three centuries, is one of Dublin's most beautiful open secrets and an absolute highlight of any visit. Atop its ancient stairs are beautiful dark-oak bookcases, each topped with elaborately carved and gilded gables, and crammed with 25,000 books, manuscripts and maps dating back to the 15th century. (www.marshlibrary.ie; St Patrick's Close; adult/child €5/free; ⊙9.30am-5pm Mon & Wed-Fri, from 10am Sat; 📋50, 50A, 56A from Aston Quay, 54, 54A from Burgh Quay)

Teeling Distillery
DISTILLERY

2 ⊙ MAP P100, G4

The first new distillery in Dublin for 125 years, Teeling only began production in 2015 and it will be several years before any of the distillate can be called whiskey. In the meantime, you can explore the visitor centre and taste (and buy) whiskeys from the family's other distillery on the Cooley Peninsula. (www.teelingwhiskey.com; 13-17 Newmarket; tours €15-30; ⊙10am-5.40pm; 📋27, 77A & 151 from city centre)

Irish Museum of Modern Art
MUSEUM

3 ⊙ MAP P100, B3

Ireland's most important collection of modern and contemporary Irish and international art is housed in the elegant, airy expanse of the Royal Hospital Kilmainham, designed by Sir William Robinson and built between 1684 and 1687 as a retirement home for soldiers. It fulfilled this role until 1928, after which it languished for nearly 50 years until a 1980s restoration saw it come back to life as this wonderful repository of art. (IMMA; www.imma.ie; Military Rd; admission free; ⊙11.30am-5.30pm Tue-Fri, from 10am Sat, from noon Sun, tours 1.15pm Wed, 2.30pm Sat & Sun; 📋51, 51D, 51X, 69, 78, 79 from Aston Quay, 🚆Heuston)

Roe & Co Distillery
DISTILLERY

4 ⊙ MAP P100, E2

The newest kid in Dublin's distillery district, Roe & Co took up residence in 2019 in the old Guinness Power Station, a cool brick building opposite the main brewery entrance. The emphasis here is on cocktails – after a traditional tasting you learn about flavour profiles in a mixology workshop, before heading to the bar to sample the bartender's wares. Book ahead. (www.roeandcowhiskey.com; 91 James's St; €19-25; ⊙11am-7pm, last admission 5pm; 📋123 from city centre)

Pearse Lyons Distillery
DISTILLERY

5 ⊙ MAP P100, E2

This boutique distillery opened in the former St James' Church in the summer of 2017, distilling small-batch, craft Irish whiskey. You have a choice of three tours:

Pearse Lyons Distillery

the Trilogy tour, which includes a distillery visit, a tour of St James' graveyard and a three-whiskey tasting; the Signature Tour, which has four tastings; and the Legacy Tour, where you get to sample five whiskies, including a five-year-old single malt. (📞01-825 2244; www. pearselyonsdistillery.com; 121-122 James's St; guided tours €20-30; 🚌21A, 51B, 78, 78A, 123 from Fleet St)

St Audoen's Church of Ireland CHURCH

6 ◉ MAP P100, G2

Two churches, side by side, each bearing the same name, a tribute to St Audoen, the 7th-century bishop of Rouen (aka Ouen) and patron saint of the Normans. They built the older of the two, the Church of Ireland, between 1181 and 1212, and today it is the only medieval church in Dublin still in use. A free 30-minute guided tour departs every 30 minutes from 9.30am to 4.45pm. The newer, bigger, 19th-century **Catholic St Audoen's** (🕙Mass 1.15 & 7pm Mon-Fri, 6pm Sat, 9.30am, 11am, 12.30 & 6pm Sun) is attached. (📞01-677 0088; www.heritageireland.ie; Cornmarket, High St; 🕙9.30am-4.45pm May-Oct; 🚌50, 50A, 56A from Aston Quay, 54, 54A from Burgh Quay)

Dublin Liberties Distillery DISTILLERY

7 ◉ MAP P100, G4

Housed in a 400-year-old building is Dublin's newest distillery venture, which opened in 2019 and cements the Liberties' newly established rep as a centre for whiskey production. There's a standard tour, where you learn about the distilling process and finish with a tasting of three whiskies – the Dubliner, the Dublin Liberties and the Dead Rabbit – although these have all been distilled elsewhere as it'll be at least three years before any of the distillate can be called whiskey. (https://thedld.com; 33 Mill St; adult/child €16/14; ☺9.30am-6pm Mon-Thu, to 7pm Fri & Sat, 11am-7pm Sun Apr-Aug, 10am-5.30pm Mon-Sat, from 11am Sun Sep-Mar; ☐49, 54A from city centre)

Eating

Assassination Custard CAFE €

8 ⊗ MAP P100, H4

It doesn't look like much, but this is one of the tastiest treats in town. The small menu changes daily – think roasted cauliflower with toasted dukkah, or broccoli with spicy Italian *nduja* (pork salami) and Toonsbridge ricotta. If you're feeling really adventurous, try the tripe sandwich. The name comes from a phrase coined by Samuel Beckett. (☏087 997 1513; www.facebook.com/assassinationcustard; 19 Kevin St; mains €7-9; ☺noon-3pm Tue-Fri; ☐all city centre)

Coke Lane Pizza PIZZA €

Excellent sourdough pizzas served fresh from the hatch on the terrace of Luckys pub (see 17 ☺ Map p100, G3). Visit before 7pm and you can get pizza and a pint (or a glass of wine) for €13 – possibly the best bargain in town. (www.cokelanepizza.com; 78 Meath St; pizzas €10-13; ☺5-

11pm Sun-Fri, from 2pm Sat; ☐13, 40, 123 from city centre)

1837 Bar & Brasserie BRASSERIE €

9 ⊗ MAP P100, E3

This lunchtime brasserie serves tasty dishes, from really fresh oysters to an insanely good Guinness burger, with skin-on fries and red-onion chutney. The drinks menu features a range of Guinness variants such as West Indian porter and Golden Ale. Highly recommended for lunch if you're visiting the museum. (☏01-471 4602; www.guinness-storehouse.com; Guinness Storehouse, St James's Gate; mains €14-18; ☺noon-3pm; ☐21A, 51B, 78, 78A, 123 from Fleet St, ☐James's)

Legit Coffee Co CAFE €

10 ⊗ MAP P100, F3

A rare trendy spot in the middle of one of Dublin's most traditional streets, Legit is full of stripped-down wood, speciality teas and strong espresso. A great spot to enjoy a toasted brioche or a filling sandwich. (www.legitcoffeeco.com; 1 Meath Mart, Meath St; mains €5-12; ☺8am-4pm Mon-Fri, from 9.30am Sat; ☐James's)

Fumbally CAFE €

11 ⊗ MAP P100, H4

A bright, airy warehouse cafe that serves healthy breakfasts, salads and sandwiches – while the occasional guitarist strums away in the corner. Its Wednesday dinner (tapas from €6) is an organic, locally sourced exploration of the cuisines of the world that is insanely popular with locals; advance bookings suggested. (☑01-529 8732; www. thefumbally.ie; Fumbally Lane; mains €7-12; ☺8am-5pm Tue-Fri, from 10am Sat, plus 7-9.30pm Wed; ☐49, 54A from city centre)

Clanbrassil House IRISH €€

12 ✖ MAP P100, G6

With an emphasis on family-style sharing plates, this intimate restaurant consistently turns out exquisite dishes, cooked on a charcoal grill. Think rib-eye with bone marrow and anchovy, or ray wing with capers and brown shrimp butter. The hash brown chips are a thing of glory, too. Order the full feast menu (€50) for the chef's choice. (☑01-453 9786; www.clanbrassilhouse.com; 6 Upper Clanbrassil St; mains €19-28; ☺5-10pm Tue-Fri, 11.30am-2.30pm & 5-10pm Sat; ☐9, 16, 49, 54A from city centre)

Variety Jones IRISH €€

13 ✖ MAP P100, G2

With a simple menu of stellar dishes, Variety Jones is offering some of the most exciting cooking in Dublin. Dishes are cooked on a hearth for a hearty, smoky flavour, and there's an emphasis on sharing dishes. Booking essential. (☑01-454 4976; www.varietyjones.ie; 78 Thomas St; mains €14-30; ☺5.30-10pm Tue-Sat; ☐13, 40, 123 from city centre)

Drinking

Old Royal Oak PUB

14 ☺ MAP P100, B3

Locals are fiercely protective of this gorgeous traditional pub, which opened in 1845 to serve the patrons and staff of the Royal Hospital (now the Irish Museum of Modern Art). The clientele has changed, but everything else remains the same, which makes this one of the nicest pubs in the city in which to enjoy a few pints. (11 Kilmainham Lane; ☺5pm-midnight Mon-Thu, 3pm-1am Fri, 12.30pm-1am Sat, 12.30-11pm Sun; ☐68, 79 from city centre)

Drop Dead Twice BAR

15 ☺ MAP P100, G3

The taproom downstairs is a great little boozer, but upstairs things are a bit jazzier with the BYO cocktail lounge. Bring a bottle of your favourite spirit, pay for a sitting of two/three hours (€25/35) and the bartenders will whizz you up cocktails using their extensive ingredients. We've seen cocktails infused with peat smoke, homemade bitters and even bacon. (www.dropdeadtwice. com; 18/19 Francis St; ☺5-11.30pm Tue-Thu, to 12.30am Fri, noon-12.30am Sat, noon-11pm Sun; ☐51B, 51C, 78A, 123 from city centre)

Fourth Corner BAR

16 ☺ MAP P100, H4

Back in the day, this little intersection in the Liberties was known

Distillery District

The Liberties might be dominated by the world-famous Guinness brewery, but Dublin's most traditional neighbourhood has rediscovered whiskey. In 2015 the Teeling Distillery (p102) reopened after a hiatus of nearly 200 years (the original on nearby Marrowbone Lane operated between 1782 and 1822), followed in 2017 by the opening of the Pearse Lyons Distillery (p102), which began operations in the former St James's Church on James St. Pearse Lyons and his wife Deirdre own a brewery and distillery in Kentucky (as well as the giant animal nutrition company Alltech), but this new project is close to Lyons' heart as his own grandfather is buried in the church's graveyard. In 2019 two more distilleries opened: the Dublin Liberties Distillery (p103) and Roe & Co (p102), whose owners Diageo also own Guinness.

The boilerplate tours are all similar: you learn about the distilling process and finish with a tasting; for extra you get a master distiller experience, which includes more detail and more whiskey. The problem with all the new arrivals is that it takes a minimum of three years before anything they make can be officially called whiskey, so until the casks have reached maturation the whiskey you're tasting is a blend of something distilled elsewhere, usually the Cooley Distillery in County Louth.

as the Four Corners of Hell, with a rowdy pub on each corner (and brawls on the streets in-between). Nowadays, things are a bit more sedate, and this swish bar is a great place for a pint. You can get **Dublin Pizza Company** (📞01-561 1714; www.dublinpizzacompany.ie; pizzas €9-13) delivered here, too. (www.fourthcorner.ie; 50 Patrick St; ⏰4-11.30pm Mon-Thu, 1pm-12.30am Fri, 2pm-12.30am Sat & Sun; 🚌49, 54A from city centre)

Lucky's

BAR

17 🗺 MAP P100, G3

A bright spot on a street that draws the crowds after dark, Lucky's comes with sleek wood and a nice selection of local craft beer. Coke Lane Pizza (p104) has also set up shop in the beer garden to cook fresh pizzas all night. (📞01-556 2397; www.luckys.ie; 78 Meath St; ⏰11.30am-midnight Mon-Thu, to 1am Fri, 1pm-1am Sat, 1-11.30pm Sun; 🚌13, 40, 123 from city centre)

Open Gate Brewery
BREWERY

18 MAP P100, E2

If the Storehouse (p92) isn't enough to satisfy the beer lover in you, try the results of the Guinness experimental brewery. You must book ahead online and each ticket comes with a sample tasting board. Quiz the brewers while you're there and relish the unique chance to taste beers that will probably never leave the building. (☎01-471 2455; www.guinnessopengate.com; St James's Gate; ◷5.30-10.30pm Thu & Fri, 2-8pm Sat; ☒13, 40, 123 from city centre)

Arthur's
PUB

19 MAP P100, E2

Given its location, Arthur's could easily be a cheesy tourist trap, and plenty of Guinness Storehouse (p92) visitors do pass through the doors tempted by another taste of the black stuff. Instead it's a friendly, cosy bar with a menu full of good comfort food. Best visited in winter so you get the full benefit of the roaring fireplace and soft candlelight. (☎01-402 0914; www.arthurspub.ie; 28 Thomas St; ◷11am-11.30pm Mon-Thu, to 12.30am Fri & Sat, to 11pm Sun; ☒21A, 51B, 78, 78A, 123 from Fleet St, ☒James's)

Fallon's
PUB

20 MAP P100, G4

A fabulously old-fashioned bar that has been serving a great pint of Guinness since the end of the 17th century. Prizefighter Dan Donnelly, the only boxer ever to be knighted, was head bartender here in 1818. A local's local. (☎01-454 2801; 129 The Coombe; ◷10.30am-11.30pm Mon-Thu, to 12.30am Fri & Sat, 12.30-11pm Sun; ☒51B, 123, 206 from city centre)

Entertainment

Vicar Street
LIVE MUSIC

21 MAP P100, G3

Vicar Street is a midsized venue with a capacity of around 1000, spread between the table-serviced group-seating downstairs and a theatre-style balcony. It offers a varied program, from comedy to soul, jazz, folk and world music. (☎01-454 5533; www.vicarstreet.com; 58-59 Thomas St; tickets €25-60; ◷7pm-midnight; ☒13, 49, 54A, 56A from city centre)

Walking Tour 🚶

Wander the Wilds of Phoenix Park

The hugely impressive 709 hectares that comprise Phoenix Park are not just a magnificent playground for all kinds of sport, from running to polo, but are also home to the president of Ireland, the American ambassador and a shy herd of fallow deer. The park is also where you'll find Europe's oldest zoo. How's that for a place to stretch your legs?

Walk Facts

Start Parkgate St entrance

End Magazine Fort

Length 14.5km; three hours

🚌 25, 26, 46A, 66/66A/66B, 67 and 69 from the city centre.

🚊 Luas Red Line to Heuston Station.

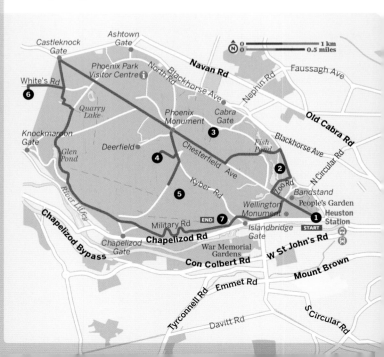

❶ Parkgate St Entrance

Chesterfield Ave runs northwest through the **park** (www.phoenixpark.ie) to the Castleknock Gate. The 63m-high Wellington Monument obelisk was completed in 1861; nearby is the People's Garden, dating from 1864, and the bandstand in the Hollow.

❷ A Lion's Roar

The 28-hectare **Dublin Zoo** (www.dublinzoo.ie; adult/child/family €19.50/14/53; ⏰9.30am-6pm Mar-Sep, to dusk Oct-Feb; 👶) opened in 1831, making it one of the oldest zoos in the world. It's been hugely developed, but its lion-breeding programme dates back to 1857 – including an offspring of the lion that roars at the start of MGM films.

❸ The Presidential Pile

If the 1751 Palladian mansion **Áras an Uachtaráin** (www.president. ie; admission free; ⏰guided tours hourly 10.30am-3.30pm Sat), the official residence of the Irish president, seems vaguely familiar, it's because it was James Hoban's inspiration for the White House. Take the free one-hour tour.

❹ A Cross Fit for a Pope

Across Chesterfield Ave – and easily visible from the road – is the massive Papal Cross, which marks the site where Pope John Paul II preached to 1.25 million people in 1979 (and where Pope Francis said Mass to far fewer in 2018). In the centre of the park, the Phoenix Monument, erected by Lord Chesterfield in 1747, looks so unlike a phoenix that it's often referred to as the Eagle Monument.

❺ Fifteen Acres

The huge expanse of greenery south of the cross – where you're most likely to see the deer – is known as the Fifteen Acres, though it's actually much bigger than that. At weekends, the pitches fill with football (soccer) teams. On the other side of the cross is the old chief secretary's lodge, Deerfield, now the official residence of the US ambassador.

❻ Out to Farmleigh

Towards the Castleknock Gate is this fine Georgian-Victorian **pile** (www.farmleigh.ie; adult/child €8/4; ⏰10am-5.30pm, last entry 4.30pm, by guided tour only), originally designed by James Gandon. Only the ground floor, with a fantastic library and glass conservatory, is on view, but the vast pleasure gardens, with lake and walled and Japanese gardens, are delightful for a stroll.

❼ And Back into the City

Take the side road around the southern perimeter. Back towards the Parkgate St entrance is the Magazine Fort. It provided target practice during the 1916 Easter Rising, and was raided by the IRA in 1940, when the entire ammunition reserve of the Irish army was nabbed.

Explore ◈

North of the Liffey

Grittier than its more genteel southside counterpart, the area immediately north of the River Liffey offers a fascinating mix of 18th-century grandeur, traditional city life and the multicultural melting pot that is contemporary Dublin. Beyond its widest, most elegant boulevard you'll find art museums and whiskey museums, bustling markets and some of the best ethnic eateries in town.

The Short List

○ **Hugh Lane Gallery (p112)** *Nodding sagely at the exquisite collection of modern and contemporary art.*

○ **Jameson Distillery Bow Street (p119)** *Sampling a snifter of whiskey after discovering how it's made in this converted distillery museum.*

○ **14 Henrietta Street (p118)** *Renovated Georgian mansion that tells the story of Dublin, from grandeur through difficult times.*

○ **National Museum of Ireland – Decorative Arts & History (p118)** *Wandering about the glorious yard of Collins Barracks, without forgetting the outstanding collection itself.*

Getting There & Around

🚌 All city-centre buses stop on O'Connell St or the nearby quays.

🚊 The Luas runs east–west parallel to the Liffey from The Point to Heuston Station.

🚆 The DART runs from Connolly Station northeast to Clontarf Rd.

North of the Liffey Map on p116

Garden of Remembrance (p115) TRABANTOS / SHUTTERSTOCK ©

Top Experience 📸

Appreciate Modern Art at Hugh Lane Gallery

Whatever reputation Dublin may have as a repository of top-class art is in large part due to the collection at this magnificent gallery, home to impressionist masterpieces, the best of modern Irish work from 1950 onward, and the actual studio of Francis Bacon.

◉ MAP P116, F2

📞 01-222 5550

www.hughlane.ie

22 N Parnell Sq

admission free

🕑 9.45am-6pm Tue-Thu, to 5pm Fri, 10am-5pm Sat, 11am-5pm Sun

Francis Bacon Studio

Impressionist masterpieces notwithstanding, the gallery's most popular exhibit is the Francis Bacon Studio (pictured), which was painstakingly moved, in all its shambolic mess, from 7 Reece Mews, South Kensington, London, where the Dublin-born artist (1909–92) lived for 31 years. The display features some 80,000 items madly strewn about the place, including slashed canvases, the last painting he was working on.

The Hugh Lane Bequest

The collection (known as the Hugh Lane Bequest 1917) was split in a complicated 1959 settlement that sees the eight masterpieces divided into two groups and alternated between Dublin and London every six years. The paintings currently on show (until 2021) are *Les Parapluies* (The Umbrellas) by Auguste Renoir, *Portrait of Eva Gonzales* by Edouard Manet, *Jour d'Été* (Summer's Day) by Berthe Morisot and *View of Louveciennes* by Camille Pissarro.

Sean Scully Gallery

The gallery's newest wing (opened 2006) is a two-storey extension with – on the ground floor – a gallery dedicated to seven abstract paintings by Irish-born Sean Scully, probably Ireland's most famous living painter. Elsewhere in the new wing is work by other contemporary Irish artists including Dorothy Cross, Brian Maguire and Norah McGuinness.

Stained Glass Gallery

Just by the main reception desk is the Stained Glass gallery, whose highlight is Harry Clarke's wonderful *The Eve of St Agnes* (1924). His masterpiece is made up of 22 separate panels, each a depiction of a stanza of John Keats' eponymous poem about the doomed love between Madeline and Porphyro, who cannot meet because their families are sworn enemies.

★ **Top Tips**

o The gallery has developed a decent app and a growing online catalogue of its collection, which allows you to search by artist and view their work before (or after) your visit.

✕ **Take a Break**

o You can round off a satisfying visit with lunch in the superb **cafe** (☏01-874 1903; www.hughlane.ie; 22 N Parnell Sq; mains €6-14; ◷9.45am-5.45pm Tue-Thu, to 4.45pm Fri, 10am-4.45pm Sat, 11am-4.45pm Sun; 🚌3, 10, 11, 13, 16, 19, 22 from city centre) in the basement, before making a stop in the well-stocked gift shop.

★ **Getting Here**

🚌7, 11, 13, 16, 38, 40, 46A, 123 from city centre

Walking Tour 🥾

Take a Walk on the Northside

North of the river, the graceful avenue that is O'Connell St introduces visitors to what was once the city's most desirable neighbourhood. Georgian Dublin was born here, on Parnell and Mountjoy squares; it played a starring role in the nation's struggle for independence; and it's still home to some of the best museums in town.

Walk Facts

Start Mountjoy Sq
End St Michan's Church
Length 2.5km; two hours

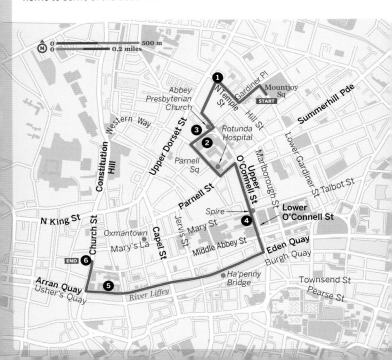

❶ St George's Church

From Mountjoy Square, take a left at the northwestern corner and walk down Gardiner Pl, turning right onto North Temple St. Up ahead is the fine but now deconsecrated (and scaffolded) Georgian **St George's Church** (closed to public), designed by architect Francis Johnston.

❷ Garden of Remembrance

Take a left onto Hardwicke St and left again onto North Frederick St, past the **Abbey Presbyterian Church** (1864). Take a peek inside the **Garden of Remembrance** (www.heritageireland.ie; ☉8.30am-6pm Apr-Sep, 9.30am-4pm Oct-Mar), opened in 1966 to commemorate the 50th anniversary of the 1916 Easter Rising.

❸ Hugh Lane Gallery

Facing the park is the excellent Hugh Lane Gallery (p112), home to some of the best modern art in Europe. The southern part of Parnell Sq is occupied by the Rotunda Hospital, a wonderful example of public architecture in the Georgian style.

❹ General Post Office

Head south down O'Connell St, passing by the 120m-high Spire. On the western side of O'Connell St, the stunning neoclassical **General Post Office** (www.anpost. ie; ☉8am-8pm Mon-Sat) towers over the street – this was the operational headquarters for the 1916 Easter Rising: you can still see the bullet holes in the columns.

❺ Four Courts

When you hit the river, turn right and walk along the boardwalk until you reach the Ha'Penny Bridge, named for the charge levied on those who used it. Continue west along Ormond Quay to one of James Gandon's Georgian masterpieces, the **Four Courts** (☎01-886 8000; Inns Quay; admission free; ☉9am-5pm Mon-Fri), home to the most important law courts in Ireland.

❻ St Michan's Church

Finally take a right onto Church St to admire **St Michan's Church** (adult/child €6/4; ☉10am-12.45pm & 2-4.45pm Mon-Fri, 10am-12.45pm Sat), a beautiful Georgian construction with grisly vaults populated by the remains of the long departed.

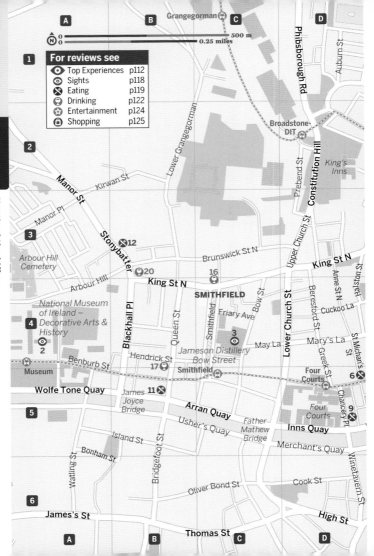

Grangegorman

Phibsborough Rd

For reviews see

⊙ Top Experiences	p112
⊚ Sights	p118
✕ Eating	p119
⊖ Drinking	p122
✪ Entertainment	p124
⛉ Shopping	p125

0 — 500 m
0 — 0.25 miles

Broadstone-
DIT

Constitution Hill

King's
Inns

Manor St

Kirwan St

Lower Grangegorman

Prebend St

Upper Church St

Manor Pl

Stonybatter

✕12

Brunswick St N

King St N

Arbour Hill
Cemetery

⊙20

King St N

SMITHFIELD

16
⊙

Bow St

Lower Church St

Anne St N

Cuckoo La

St Michan's St
Halston St

Beresford St

Arbour Hill

Blackhall Pl

Queen St

Smithfield

Friary Ave

Mary's La

Greek St

National Museum
of Ireland –
Decorative Arts &
History

⊙
2

Benburb St

Hendrick St

17⊖

3
⊙
Jameson Distillery
Bow Street

May La

Four
Courts

⊟
Museum

Smithfield

Four
Courts

6
✕

Chancery Pl

Wolfe Tone Quay

James 11✕
Joyce
Bridge

Arran Quay

Father
Mathew
Bridge

Inns Quay

9
✕

Island St

Usher's Quay

Winetavern St

Watling St

Bridgefoot St

Merchant's Quay

Bonham St

Oliver Bond St

Cook St

High St

James's St

Thomas St

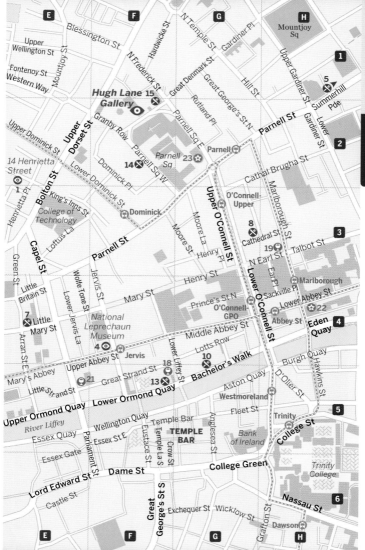

North of the Liffey

Sights

14 Henrietta Street   MUSEUM

1 MAP P116, E2

Explore one of Dublin's Georgian townhouses, carefully restored to gently peel back layers of complex social history over 250 years. Part museum, part community archive, it covers the magnificent elegance of upper-class life in the 1740s to the destitution of the early 20th century, when the house was occupied by 100 tenants living in near squalor. Access is by 75-minute guided tour only, which means visitors get the benefit of lots of interesting detail. (☏01-524 0383; www.14henriettastreet.ie; 14 Henrietta St; adult/child €9/6; ⓢtours

hourly 10am-4pm Wed-Sat, from noon Sun; 🚌9, 13, 16, 40 from city centre)

National Museum of Ireland – Decorative Arts & History   MUSEUM

2 MAP P116, A4

Once the world's largest military barracks, this splendid early neoclassical grey-stone building on the Liffey's northern banks was completed in 1704 according to the design of Thomas Burgh (he of Trinity College's Old Library). It is now home to the Decorative Arts & History collection of the National Museum of Ireland, with a range of superb permanent exhibits ranging from a history of the 1916 Easter Rising to the work of iconic Irish designer Eileen Gray

14 Henrietta Street

ANNEMARIE MCCARTHY / LONELY PLANET ©

(1878–1976). (www.museum.ie; Benburb St; admission free; 10am-5pm Tue-Sat, from 2pm Sun; 25, 66, 67, 90 from city centre, Museum)

Jameson Distillery Bow Street

MUSEUM

3 ◉ MAP P116, C4

Smithfield's biggest draw is devoted to *uisce beatha* (ish-kuh ba-ha, 'the water of life'); which is Irish for whiskey. To its more serious devotees, that is precisely what whiskey is, although they may be put off by the slickness of this museum (occupying part of the old distillery that stopped production in 1971), which shepherds visitors through a compulsory tour of the recreated factory (the tasting at the end is a lot of fun) and into the ubiquitous gift shop. (www.jamesonwhiskey.com; Bow St; adult/student/child €19/18/11, masterclasses €60; 10am-5pm Mon-Sat, from 10.30am Sun; 25, 66, 67, 90 from city centre, Smithfield)

National Leprechaun Museum

MUSEUM

4 ◉ MAP P116, F4

Ostensibly designed as a child-friendly museum of Irish folklore, this is really a romper room for kids sprinkled with bits of fairy tale. Which is no bad thing, even if the picture of the leprechaun painted here is more Lucky Charms and Walt Disney than sinister creature of pre-Christian mythology. (www.leprechaunmuseum.ie; Twilfit House, Jervis St; adult/

child €16/10, Darkland Tour €18; 10am-6.30pm, also 7-8.30pm Fri & Sat; all city centre, Jervis)

Eating

Da Mimmo's

ITALIAN €

5 ✕ MAP P116, H1

The son of the original owners converted what was once a traditional fish-and-chip shop into this sit-down restaurant, now serving some of the best Italian food in the city. Everything here – from the Caprese salad to the lasagne – is as authentic as if you were dining in Tino's hometown of Casalattico (between Naples and Rome). (01-856 1714; www.damimmo.ie; 148 North Strand Rd; mains €12-24; noon-10pm; 53 from Talbot St)

Fegan's 1924

CAFE €

6 ✕ MAP P116, D5

A slice of rural Ireland in the city centre: this wonderful cafe is all distressed furniture and rustic charm, but there's nothing old-fashioned about the food and coffee. Fluffy scrambled eggs, perfectly made French toast and excellent brews...this is a place designed for lingering. Weekends also feature 40-minute creative workshops for kids (€6 each). No cash; cards only. (01-872 2788; www.fegans1924.com; 13 Chancery St; mains €6-9; 7.30am-4pm Mon-Fri, from 11am Sat & Sun; ; 25, 66, 67, 90 from city centre, Four Courts)

Street Smart

By day, O'Connell St is a bustle of activity, with shoppers, hawkers, walkers and others going about their business. At night, however, it can be a different story, as alcohol and drugs can give the street an air of menace and, sadly, the odd spot of trouble.

Dubliners are sick of complaining that the police presence is virtually nonexistent here (the police counter by declaring they're sick of their valuable resources constantly being cut), so you'll have to keep your wits about you.

Oxmantown CAFE €

7 ⊗ MAP P116, E4

Delicious breakfasts and excellent sandwiches make this cafe one of the standout places for daytime eating on the north side of the Liffey. Locally baked bread, coffee supplied by Cloud Picker (Dublin's only microroastery) and meats sourced from Irish farms are the ingredients, but it's the way it's all put together that makes it so worthwhile. (www.oxmantown.com; 16 Mary's Abbey, City Markets; sandwiches €6.50; ⏰8am-4pm Mon-Fri; 🚊Four Courts, Jervis)

M&L CHINESE €

8 ⊗ MAP P116, G3

Beyond the plain frontage and the cheap-looking decor is Dublin's best Chinese restaurant...by some distance. It's usually full of Chinese customers, who come for the authentic Szechuan-style cuisine – spicier than Cantonese and with none of the concessions usually made to Western palates (no prawn crackers or curry chips). (📞01-874 8038; www.mlchineserestaurant.com; 13/14 Cathedral St; mains €11-20; ⏰11.30am-10pm Mon-Sat, from noon Sun; 🚊all city centre)

Legal Eagle IRISH €€

9 ⊗ MAP P116, D5

With the aesthetic of an old Dublin pub, combined with a kitchen churning out top-notch comfort food, this is one of Dublin's best new restaurants. There's a wood oven for potato flatbreads topped with Toonsbridge mozzarella and oxtail, and the retro-influenced Sunday menu is a contender for the best roast in town. (📞01-555 2971; www.thelegaleagle.ie; 1/2 Chancery Pl; mains €22-30; ⏰9.30am-4pm Mon & Tue, to 10pm Wed-Fri, noon-10pm Sat, noon-9pm Sun; 🚊Four Courts)

Terra Madre ITALIAN €€

10 ⊗ MAP P116, G4

It would be easy to walk past the entrance to this basement restaurant. But if you did, you'd be missing out on some of the most authentic Italian food in Dublin. The menu is small and constantly changing, but will always feature a few pastas (like pappardelle with duck ragu) and *secondi* (like Tuscan tripe). Exceptional. (📞01-873 5300; www.terramadre.ie; 13A Bachelor's Walk; mains €15-21; 🕐12.30-3pm & 5-10pm; 🚇all city centre)

Fish Shop   SEAFOOD €€

11 ✕ MAP P116, B5

The menu changes daily at this tiny restaurant (it has only 16 seats) to reflect what's good and fresh, but you'll have to trust them: your only choice is a four-course or tasting menu. One day you might fancy line-caught mackerel with a green sauce, another day slip sole with caper butter. Maybe the best seafood restaurant in town. (📞01-430 8594; www.fish-shop.ie; 6 Queen St; 4-course set menu €45; 🕐6-10pm Wed-Sat; 🚌25, 25A, 66, 67 from city centre, 🚇Smithfield)

L Mulligan Grocer   IRISH €€

12 ✕ MAP P116, B3

It's a great traditional pub, but the main reason to come here is for the food, all sourced locally and made by expert hands. The menu includes an excellent free-range chicken Kiev, and a hefty artisanal Scotch egg (along with a vegetarian counterpart). There is an extensive selection of beers and whiskeys on offer, too. (📞01-670 9889; www.lmulligangrocer.com; 18 Stoneybatter; mains €17-23; 🕐4-10pm Mon-Fri, from 12.30pm Sat, 12.30-9pm Sun; 🚌25, 25A, 66, 67 from city centre, 🚇Museum)

Winding Stair (p122)

ANDREW MONTGOMERY / LONELY PLANET ©

North of the Liffey Eating

Winding Stair

IRISH €€

13 ✖ MAP P116, F5

In a beautiful Georgian building that once housed the city's most beloved bookshop – the ground floor still is one (p125) – the Winding Stair's conversion to elegant restaurant has been faultless. The wonderful Irish menu (potted crab, haddock poached in milk, steamed mussels and gorgeous fat chips) coupled with an excellent wine list makes for a memorable meal. (📞01-873 7320; www.winding-stair.com; 40 Lower Ormond Quay; 2-course lunch €24, mains €25-32; ⏱noon-3.30pm & 5.30-10.30pm; 🚌all city centre)

Mr Fox

IRISH €€€

14 ✖ MAP P116, F2

In a gorgeous Georgian townhouse on Parnell Sq, the fantastic Mr Fox is cooking some of the finest food in the city. The plates celebrate Irish ingredients with a cheeky twist – think venison with black pudding, chestnut and blackberries, or pheasant with lentils and Toulouse sausage. A Michelin star can't be too far away. (📞01-874 7778; www.mrfox.ie; 38 W Parnell Sq; mains €20-30; ⏱noon-2pm & 5-9.30pm Tue-Sat; 🚌Parnell)

Chapter One

IRISH €€€

15 ✖ MAP P116, F2

Flawless haute cuisine and a relaxed, welcoming atmosphere make this Michelin-starred restaurant in the basement of the Dublin Writers Museum our choice for the best dinner experience in town. The food is French-inspired contemporary Irish; the menus change regularly; and the service is top-notch. The three-course pre-theatre menu (€44) is great if you're going to the Gate (p124) around the corner. (📞01-873 2266; www.chapteronerestaurant.com; 18 N Parnell Sq; 2-course lunch €36.50, 4-course dinner €80; ⏱12.30-2pm Fri, 5-10.30pm Tue-Sat; 🚌3, 10, 11, 13, 16, 19, 22 from city centre)

Drinking

Cobblestone

PUB

16 🚇 MAP P116, C4

It advertises itself as a 'drinking pub with a music problem', which is an apt description for this Smithfield stalwart – although the traditional music sessions that run throughout the week can hardly be described as problematic. Wednesday's Balaclava session (from 7.30pm) is for any musician who is learning an instrument, with musician Síomha Mulligan on hand to teach. (www.cobblestonepub.ie; N King St; ⏱4.30-11.30pm Mon-Thu, 2pm-12.30am Fri & Sat, 1.30-11pm Sun; 🚇Smithfield)

Token

BAR

17 🚇 MAP P116, B4

This arcade-style bar is fitted out with retro video games and pinball machines. As well as a full bar, the restaurant serves generous portions of innovative, gourmet

One Foot in the Grave

A contender for best pub in Dublin is **John Kavanagh's** (Gravediggers; ☎ 01-830 7978; www.facebook.com/JohnKavanaghTheGravediggers; 1 Prospect Sq; ⏰ 10.30am-11.30pm Mon-Thu, to midnight Fri & Sat, to 11pm Sun; 🚌 13, 19, 19A from O'Connell St) of Glasnevin, more commonly known as the Gravediggers because the employees from the adjacent cemetery had a secret serving hatch so that they could drink on the job. Founded in 1833, it is reputedly Dublin's oldest family-owned pub: the current owners are the sixth generation of Kavanaghs to be in charge. Inside, it's as traditional a boozer as you could hope: stone floors, lacquered wooden wall panels and all. In summer the green of the square is full of drinkers basking in the sun, while inside the hardened locals ensure that ne'er a hint of sunshine disturbs some of the best Guinness in town. An absolute classic.

fast food. Book ahead for groups of more than four if you want to eat. Over 18s only. (☎ 01-532 2699; www.tokendublin.ie; 72-74 Queen St, Smithfield; ⏰ 4-11pm; 🚌 25, 26, 37, 39, 66, 67, 69, 70, 79A from city centre, 🚊 Smithfield, Red Line)

Yamamori Tengu CLUB

18 MAP P116, F5

These two floors are the sweaty home to a mix of house, techno, soul and disco. There's lots of space to dance, a great sound system and a bar serving cocktails and Japanese beers. When your feet are sore, chill out in the bamboo smoking area. Find it through the back of **Yamamori Sushi** (38-39 Lower Ormond Quay) when open or from Great Strand St. (☎ 01-558 8405; www.yamamori.ie; 37 Great Strand St; ⏰ 6-11.30pm Wed & Thu, to 3am Fri & Sat; 🚌 all city centre)

Confession Box PUB

19 MAP P116, H3

This historic pub is popular with tourists and locals alike. Run by some of the friendliest bar staff you're likely to meet, it's also a good spot in which to brush up on your local history: the pub was a favourite spot of Michael Collins, one of the leaders in the fight for Irish independence. (☎ 01-874 7339; www.c11407968.wixsite.com/ryan; 88 Marlborough St; ⏰ 11am-11pm Mon-Fri, 10am-midnight Sat & Sun; 🚊 Abbey)

Walsh's PUB

20 MAP P116, B3

If the snug is free, a drink in Walshs is about as pure a traditional experience as you'll have in any pub in the city; if it isn't, you'll have to make do with the old-fashioned bar, where the friendly staff and brilliant clientele (a mix of locals and trendsetting imports) are a treat. A proper Dublin pub. (www.walshsstoneybatter.ie; 6 Stoneybatter; ☺3-11pm Mon-Thu, to 12.30am Fri & Sat, 3-11pm Sun; 🚌25, 25A, 66, 67 from city centre, 🚊Museum)

Pantibar
GAY & LESBIAN

21 🏳️‍🌈 MAP P116, E5

A raucous, fun gay bar owned by Rory O'Neill, aka Panti Bliss, star of 2015's acclaimed documentary *The Queen of Ireland*, about the struggle for equality that climaxes in the historic marriage referendum of May 2015. The bar has since become a place of LGBTIQ+ pilgrimage – and no-holds-barred enjoyment. Its own brew, Panti's Pale Ale, is a gorgeous beer. (www.pantibar.com; 7-8 Capel St; ☺4-11.30pm Mon-Thu, to 12.30am Fri & Sat, to 11pm Sun; 🚌all city centre)

Entertainment

Abbey Theatre
THEATRE

22 ⭐ MAP P116, H4

Ireland's national theatre was founded by WB Yeats in 1904 and was a central player in the development of a consciously native cultural identity. Expect to see a mix of homegrown theatre from Irish playwrights, as well as touring performances from around the world. (📞01-878 7222; www.abbeytheatre.ie; Lower Abbey St; 🚌all city centre, 🚊Abbey)

Gate Theatre
THEATRE

23 ⭐ MAP P116, G2

The city's most elegant theatre, housed in a late 18th-century building, features a generally unflappable repertory of classic

---

Croke Park Experience

The Gaelic Athletic Association (GAA) considers itself not just the governing body of a bunch of Irish games but also the stout defender of a cultural identity that is ingrained in Ireland's sense of self. To get an idea of just how important the GAA is, a visit to the **Croke Park Experience** (www.crokepark.ie; Clonliffe Rd, New Stand, Croke Park; adult/child museum €7/6, museum & tour €14/9; ☺9.30am-6pm Mon-Sat, 10.30am-5pm Sun Jun-Aug, 9.30am-5pm Mon-Sat, 10.30am-5pm Sun Sep-May; 🚌3, 11, 11A, 16, 16A, 123 from O'Connell St) is a must. The twice-daily tours (except match days) of the impressive Croke Park stadium are excellent, and well worth the extra cost. The stadium's most recent attraction is the **Skyline** (www.crokepark.ie; Croke Park; adult/child €20/12; ☺half-hourly 10.30am-3.30pm Mon-Sat, from 11.30am Sun Jul & Aug, 11.30am & 2.30pm Mon-Fri, half-hourly 10.30am-2.30pm Sat, from 11.30am Sun Sep-Jun; 🚌3, 11, 11A, 16, 16A, 123 from O'Connell St), a guided tour around the stadium roof.

Irish, American and European plays. Orson Welles and James Mason played here early in their careers. Even today it is the only theatre in town where you might see established international movie stars working on their actorly credibility through a theatre run. (☎01-874 4045; www. gatetheatre.ie; 1 Cavendish Row; ⏰performances 7.30pm Tue-Fri, 2.30pm & 7.30pm Sat; 🚌all city centre)

Shopping

Winding Stair

BOOKS

This handsome old bookshop (see 13 ✖ Map p116, F5) once occupied the whole building. There's a smaller selection these days, but still some excellent quality new- and old-book perusals. (☎01-872 6576; www. winding-stair.com; 40 Lower Ormond Quay; ⏰10am-6pm Mon & Fri, to 7pm Tue-Thu & Sat, noon-6pm Sun; 🚌all city centre)

Street Food

Spend an hour or two eating and drinking your way through half a dozen or so of the city's best food vendors at **Eatyard** (https://the-eatyard.com/street-food-market; Cross Guns Bridge, Drumcondra; ⏰noon-10pm Thu-Sat, to 8pm Sun Mar-Dec; 🚌40 from city centre, 🚃Drumcondra). Now in new digs in Drumcondra, north of the city centre, there's always seasonal produce, and plenty of veggie/vegan options, as well as craft beer. The vendors rotate every few months and the market can close for a short time to accommodate this – confirm opening times online.

Explore ⊚
Docklands

The gleaming modern blocks of the Docklands – dubbed Silicon Docks – are home to digital tech giants including Google, Facebook, Twitter and LinkedIn, whose European headquarters sit tidily among the offices of finance houses and other businesses. A couple of architectural beauties – notably a theatre designed by Daniel Libeskind – stand out among the modern buildings.

The Short List

o *Jeanie Johnston (p132)* Visiting this working replica of a 19th-century 'coffin' ship.

o *Famine Memorial (p131)* Contemplating Rowan Gillespie's thought-provoking bronze statues.

o *Bord Gáis Energy Theatre (p135)* Attending a gig at this spectacular theatre designed by Daniel Libeskind.

o *Poolbeg Lighthouse (p133)* Enjoying a late-afternoon stroll down the south wall to this elegant lighthouse.

Getting There & Around

🚌 Buses 1, 47, 56A and 77A go from Dame St to the edge of Grand Canal Sq. For the northside, bus 151 goes from Bachelor's Walk to the Docklands.

🚊 The Luas Red Line terminus is at the Point Village.

🚌 The DART stops at Grand Canal Quay.

Docklands Map on p130

Samuel Beckett bridge with the Convention Centre behind (p133)

Walking Tour 🥾

The Docklands' Hidden Heritage

Bright and gleaming, the docklands may be the city's newest development – most of the buildings are barely 10 years old – but in between the shiny architectural boxes are bits of Dublin heritage, including links to the 1916 Easter Rising. Oh, and some nice bridges that will afford some pretty picture options.

Walk Facts

Start CHQ Building
End Treasury Building
Length 2km; 30 minutes

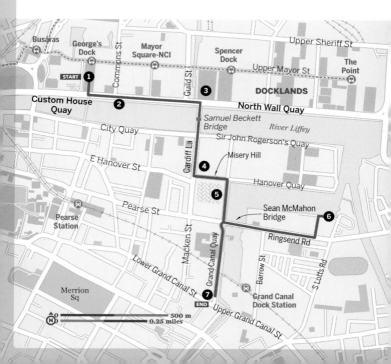

❶ Heritage & History

Explore the history of migration – and maybe your own heritage? – at the high-tech EPIC Irish Emigration Museum (p131) inside the CHQ Building, where you'll also find the Irish Family History Centre. Here you can get a personalised take on your Irish roots.

❷ Legacy of the Famine

How times have changed. In the shadow of Dublin's financial services sector is the Jeanie Johnston (p132), the 19th-century ship that transported Irish emigrants fleeing the ravages of the Famine.

❸ Going to a Convention?

You can't miss Kevin Roche's eye-catching 2010 Convention Centre, with an angled, glass-fronted atrium that has become one of the city's most distinctive buildings. Cross to the south side of the river via the Samuel Beckett Bridge, which looks like a giant wishbone.

❹ From the Rooftop Marker Bar

Walk up Cardiff Lane and turn left onto the inappropriately named Misery Hill (neither miserable nor steep). On your left, directly facing the Bord Gáis Energy Theatre, is the Marker hotel, whose rooftop bar is the trendy spot for a drink.

❺ Grand Canal Square

From your elevated vantage point, you've a fine view of the square below, which was designed by American landscape artist Martha Schwartz and opened in 2008. Its most distinctive feature is the red 'carpet' made of bright red, resin-glass paving covered with red, glowing, angled light sticks.

❻ Wakeboarding

On the eastern end of the dock is Wakedock (p133), where you can try the relatively new sport of wakeboarding – basically waterskiing while attached to an overhead cable.

❼ Rising Links & Shiny Towers

At the corner of Grand Canal and Macken sts, the Treasury Building stands where the operational HQ for the 1916 Easter Rising, Boland's Bakery, was located. Climbing the side of the building is *Aspiration,* by Rowan Gillespie, who did the Famine Memorial on Custom House Quay.

Docklands

North Circular Rd

Summerhill Pde

Ballybough Rd

Portland Row

N Strand Rd

West Rd

Church Rd

East Wall Rd

EAST WALL

St Mary's Rd

East Wall

Royal Canal

Diamond Park

Lower Sean MacDermot St

Railway St

Amiens St

Seville Pl

Commons St

Foley St

Talbot St

Lower Gardiner St

Connolly Station

Sheriff St

Connolly

Busáras

George's Dock

Lower Mayor St

Luke Kelly Bust

Lower Sheriff St

Mayor Square - NCI

Docklands

Upper Sheriff St

NORTH WALL

The Point

Spencer Dock

Upper Mayor St

Custom House

5 ⊙ Famine Memorial

3 ⊙

2 ⊙

EPIC The Irish Emigration Museum

Guild St

9 ⊙ Convention Centre

3 Arena

1 ⊙

Irish Family History Centre

6 ⊙ Jeanie Johnston

Samuel Beckett Bridge

North Wall Quay

River Liffey

3 12

13 ⊗

Tara St Station

Townsend St

City Quay

Sir John Rogerson's Quay

Cardiff La

Pearse St

E Hanover St

Lime St

Erne St Lower

Grand Canal Square

Hanover Quay

Grand Canal Docks

14 ☆ ⊙ **7**

Trinity College

4

Nassau St

Pearse Station

Erne St Upper

Pearse St

Westland Row

Lombard St

Wakedock ⊙ **8**

Ringsend Rd

Bridge St

S Lotts Rd

Fenian St

15 🔒

Macken St

Barrow St

Grand Canal Dock Station

Kildare St

Merrion Sq N

Merrion Sq

Merrion Sq S

Lower Mount St

Lower Grand Canal St

Upper Grand Canal St

11 ⊗

10 ⊗

Bath Ave

Lansdowne Rd Station

Lower Baggot St

Fitzwilliam St Lower

Herbert Pl

Haddington Rd

Northumberland Rd

National Print Museum

Shelbourne Rd

Pembroke Rd

500 m
0.25 miles

For reviews see

⊙	Sights	p131
⊗	Eating	p133
🍷	Drinking	p134
☆	Entertainment	p135
🔒	Shopping	p135

A B C D

1 2 3 4 5 6

Sights

Irish Family History Centre CULTURAL CENTRE

1 ◉ MAP P130, B3

Discover your family history with interactive screens where you can track your surname and centuries of Irish emigration. The ticket price includes a 15-minute consultation with a genealogist, but additional 30-minute and hour-long sessions are also available. You can visit as part of the EPIC exhibition or buy a separate ticket. (☎01-671 0338; www.irishfamilyhistorycentre. com; CHQ Bldg, Custom House Quay; €12.50, incl EPIC The Irish Emigration Museum €24; 30/60min genealogist consultation €45/85; ◷10am-5pm Mon-Fri, from noon Sat; 🚊George's Dock)

EPIC The Irish Emigration Museum MUSEUM

2 ◉ MAP P130, B3

This is a high-tech, interactive exploration of emigration and its effect on Ireland and the 70 million or so people spread throughout the world who claim Irish ancestry. Start your visit with a 'passport' and proceed through 20 interactive – and occasionally moving – galleries examining why they left, where they went and how they maintained their relationship with their ancestral home.

(☎01-906 0861; www.epicchq.com; CHQ Bldg, Custom House Quay; adult/child €15/7.50; ◷10am-6.45pm, last entrance 5pm; 🚊George's Dock)

Famine Memorial MEMORIAL

3 ◉ MAP P130, A3

Just east of the Custom House (p132) is one of Dublin's most thought-provoking (and photographed) examples of public art: the set of life-size bronze figures (1997) by Rowan Gillespie, and known simply as *Famine*. Designed to commemorate the ravages of the Great Hunger (1845–51), their haunted, harrowed look testifies to a journey that was both hazardous and unwelcome. (Custom House Quay; 🚊all city centre)

Luke Kelly Bust STATUE

4 ◉ MAP P130, C2

An eye-catching 2m marble bust of folk singer Luke Kelly by award-winning German artist Vera Klute stands on the street where Kelly was born in 1940. Three-thousand individual strands of patinated copper-wire make up Kelly's famous head of curly hair and wiry beard, but it's the pose that has generated most of the commentary: Klute captured Kelly with eyes firmly closed and mouth open in song – which some point out looks like he's in the throes of orgasm. (🚊Mayor Square – NCI or Spencer Dock)

STJB / SHUTTERSTOCK ©

Custom House

Custom House   LANDMARK

5 ⊙ MAP P130, A3

Georgian genius James Gandon (1743–1823) announced his arrival on the Dublin scene with this magnificent building constructed over 10 years between 1781 and 1791, just past Eden Quay at a wide stretch in the River Liffey. It's a colossal, neoclassical pile that stretches for 114m and is topped by a copper dome. (Custom House Quay; ⊙9am-5pm Mon-Fri; ⍰all city centre)

Jeanie Johnston   MUSEUM

6 ⊙ MAP P130, B3

One of the city's most original tourist attractions is an exact working replica of a 19th-century 'coffin ship', as the sailing boats that

transported starving emigrants away from Ireland during the Famine were gruesomely known – even if the original *Jeanie Johnston* suffered no deaths in 16 journeys between 1848 and 1855, carrying a total of 2500 passengers. A small on-board museum details the harrowing plight of a typical journey, which usually took around 47 days. (www.jeaniejohnston.ie; Custom House Quay; adult/student/child/family €10/9/6/28; ⊙tours hourly 10am-4pm Apr-Oct, 11am-3pm Nov-Mar; ⍰all city centre, ⍰George's Dock)

Grand Canal Square   SQUARE

7 ⊙ MAP P130, C4

This modern square was designed by American landscape artist Martha Schwartz and opened in 2008. Its most distinctive feature is the red 'carpet' made of bright red resin-glass paving covered with red glowing angled light sticks. (🚊Grand Canal Dock)

Wakedock ADVENTURE SPORTS

8 👁 MAP P130, D4

Try the relatively new sport of cable wakeboarding – waterskiing by holding on to a fixed overhead cable instead of a motorboat. You can then graduate to flips and jumps over obstacles in the water. The sport is shortlisted for the 2020 Olympics. You can also rent wetsuits (€2). (📞01-664 3883; www.wakedock.ie; Grand Canal Dock; 30min tuition adult/student €60/45; 🕙noon-8pm Tue-Fri, from 10am Sat & Sun; 🚌1, 15A, 15B, 56A, 77A from city centre, 🚊Grand Canal Dock)

Convention Centre LANDMARK

9 👁 MAP P130, C3

The angled, tube-like Convention Centre was designed by Kevin Roche in 2011. It looks its best at night, when it is lit up. (Spencer Dock, North Wall Quay; 🕙closed to the public; 🚊Mayor Square – NCI)

Eating

Juniors Deli & Cafe ITALIAN €€

10 🍴 MAP P130, D5

Cramped and easily mistaken for any old cafe, Juniors is hardly ordinary. Designed to imitate a New York deli, the food (Italian-influenced, all locally sourced produce) is delicious, the atmos-

Poolbeg Lighthouse

One of the city's most reward-ing walks follows the Great South Wall to the **Poolbeg Lighthouse** (South Wall; 🕙24hr; 🚌1, 47, 56A, 77A, 84N from city centre), that red tower visible in the middle of Dublin Bay. The lighthouse dates from 1768, but it was redesigned and re-built in 1820. To get there, take the bus to Ringsend from the city centre, and then make your way past the power station to the start of the wall (it's about 1km). It's not an especially long walk out to the lighthouse – about 800m or so – but it will give you a stunning view of the bay and the city behind you, a view best enjoyed just before sunset on a summer's evening.

phere always buzzing (it's often hard to get a table) and the ethos top-notch, which is down to the two brothers who run the place. (📞01-664 3648; www.juniors.ie; 2 Bath Ave; mains €17-26; 🕙8.30am-10.30am, noon-2.30pm & 5.30-10pm Mon-Fri, 11am-3pm & 5.30-10pm Sat, 11am-3.30pm Sun; 🚌3 from city centre, 🚊Grand Canal Dock)

Paulie's Pizza ITALIAN €€

11 🍴 MAP P130, D5

At the heart of this lovely, oc-casionally boisterous restaurant is a Neapolitan pizza oven, used to create some of the best pizzas

Grand Canal Square and the Bord Gáis Energy Theatre

in town. Margheritas, *biancas* (no tomato sauce), calzone and other Neapolitan specialities are the real treat, but there's also room for a classic New York slice and a few local creations. (www.paulies.ie; 58 Upper Grand Canal St; pizzas €13-17; ☺6-10pm Mon-Thu, noon-3pm & 6-10pm Fri, 2-10pm Sat & Sun; 🚼; 🚌3 from city centre, 🚆Grand Canal Dock)

Workshop Gastropub   IRISH €€

12 🍴 MAP P130, A3

Take a traditional pub and introduce a chef with a vision: hey presto, you've got a gastropub (surprisingly, one of the few in the city) serving burgers, *moules frites* (mussels served with French fries) and sandwiches, as well as a good range of salads. (Kennedy's; 📞01-677 0626; www.theworkshopgastropub.

com; 10 George's Quay; mains lunch €7-9, dinner €10-24; ☺noon-3pm & 5-10pm Sun-Fri, noon-12.30am Sat; 📶; 🚌all city centre, 🚆Tara St)

Drinking

John Mulligan's   PUB

13 🍺 MAP P130, A3

This brilliant old boozer is a cultural institution, established in 1782 and in this location since 1854. A drink (or more) here is like attending liquid services at a most sacred, secular shrine. John F Kennedy paid his respects in 1945, when he joined the cast of regulars that seems barely to have changed since. (www.mulligans.ie; 8 Poolbeg St; ☺noon-11.30pm Mon-Thu, 11am-12.30am Fri, 11.30am-12.30am Sat, 12.30-11pm Sun; 🚌all city centre)

Entertainment

Bord Gáis Energy Theatre

THEATRE

14 ⭐ MAP P130, C4

Forget the uninviting sponsored name: Daniel Libeskind's masterful design is a three-tiered, 2100-capacity auditorium where you're as likely to be entertained by the Bolshoi or a touring state opera as you are to see *Dirty Dancing* or Barbra Streisand. It's a magnificent venue – designed for classical, paid for by the classics. (📞01-677 7999; www.bordgaisenergytheatre.ie; Grand Canal Sq; 🚊Grand Canal Dock)

Shopping

Design Tower

ARTS & CRAFTS

15 🔒 MAP P130, C4

Housed in a 19th-century sugar refinery that was Dublin's first iron-structured building, this seven-storey design centre houses studios for around 20 local craftspeople, producing everything from Celtic-inspired jewellery to wall hangings and leather bags. Some studios are open by appointment only; check the website for details. (📞01-677 5655; www.thedesigntower.com; Pearse St; ⏰9am-5pm Mon-Fri; 🚊Grand Canal Dock)

Explore ✦

Southside

The neighbourhoods that border the southern bank of the Grand Canal are less about sights and more about the experience of affluent Dublin — dining, drinking and sporting occasions, both watching and taking part. Here are the city's most desirable neighbourhoods, especially Ballsbridge, Donnybrook and Ranelagh.

The Short List

∘ **Aviva Stadium (p143)** *Cheering on Leinster or Ireland (in either rugby or football).*

∘ **Herbert Park (p139)** *Strolling, sitting or jogging around this glorious stretch of greenery.*

∘ **Stella Theatre (p142)** *The city's fanciest cinema is a restored art deco classic.*

∘ **Southside Dining (p140)** *Dining in handsome Ranelagh or bustling Rathmines is always a treat, especially in spots like the Manifesto.*

∘ **National Print Museum (p139)** *Exploring the surprisingly interesting history of printing in Ireland at this terrific little museum.*

Getting There & Around

🚌 From the city centre, take buses 5, 7, 7A, 8, 45 or 46 to Ballsbridge; for Donnybrook bus 10A or 46; and for Rathmines bus 14 or 15.

🚌 The Luas green line serves Ranelagh from St Stephen's Green.

🚌 The DART serves Sandymount (for Bath Ave) and Lansdowne Rd.

Southside Map on p138

Aviva Stadium (p143) ABD / SHUTTERSTOCK ©

Southside

500 m
0.25 miles

Sandymount Rd
Tritonville Rd
Claremont Rd
Sandymount Ave
Serpentine Ave
Sandymount Rd
Sandyford Ave

SANDYMOUNT
BALLSBRIDGE

Bath Ave
BEGGAR'S BUSH
Lansdowne Rd
Lansdowne Station
Shelbourne Rd

Merrion Rd
Simmonscourt Rd
Sandymount Station
Anglesea St
River Dodder

National Print Museum
Northumberland Rd
Pembroke Rd
Pembroke La
Pembroke Rd

Haddington Rd
Herbert Pl
St Mary's Rd
Pembroke Rd
Elgin Rd
Clyde Rd

Herbert Park
Pembroke Park
Herbert Park

DONNYBROOK
Donnybrook Stadium
Donnybrook Rd
Belmont Ave

Lower Mount St
Merrion Sq S
Lower Baggot St
Upper Fitzwilliam St

Waterloo Rd
Heytesbury La
Morehampton Rd

Sandford Rd
Merton Dr
Anna Villa

Lower Leeson St
Upper Leeson St
Mespil Rd
Burlington Rd
Leeson Park
Leeson Park

St Stephen's Green
Iveagh Gardens
Upper Hatch St
Harcourt
Adelaide Rd
Charlemont St
Grand Pde
Charlemont
Leeson Park

RANELAGH
Ranelagh
Ranelagh Rd
North Brook Rd
Charleston Rd
Alpian Way

Cuffe St
Camden Row
Harcourt St
Lower Camden St
S Richmond St
Synge St
Heytesbury St
S Circular Rd
Grove Rd

Lower Rathmines Rd
Mount Pleasant Ave
Military Rd

RATHMINES
Leinster Rd
Castlewood Ave
Beechwood
Palmerston Rd
Belgrave Rd
Rathgar Rd

Sights

National Print Museum MUSEUM

1 MAP P138, D1

You don't have to be into printing to enjoy this quirky little museum, where personalised guided tours (11.30am daily and 2.30pm Monday to Friday) are offered in a delightfully casual and compelling way. A video looks at the history of printing in Ireland and then you wander through the various (still working) antique presses amid the smell of ink and metal. (☏01-660 3770; www.nationalprintmuseum.ie; Haddington Rd, Garrison Chapel, Beggar's Bush; admission free; ⏰9am-5pm Mon-Fri, from 2pm Sat & Sun; 🚌4, 7 from city centre, 🚉Grand Canal Dock, Lansdowne Rd)

Herbert Park PARK

2 MAP P138, D3

A gorgeous swathe of green lawns, ponds and flower beds near the Royal Dublin Society Showground (p143). Sandwiched between prosperous Ballsbridge and Donnybrook, the park runs along the River Dodder. There are tennis courts and a kids playground here too. (Ballsbridge; ⏰dawn-dusk; 🚌5, 7, 7A, 8, 45, 46 from city centre, 🚉Sandymount, Lansdowne Rd)

Southside Sights

National Print Museum

The Two Mikes

Looking for the best seafood in the city? You'll have to venture a little further south into the suburbs of Mount Merrion to **Michael's** (📞01-278 0377; www.michaels.ie; 57 Deerpark Rd; mains €18-33; ⏰noon-10pm Tue-Sat; 🚌47 from city centre), where chef Gaz Smith turns the freshest fish and shellfish into something approaching perfection. **Little Mike's**, a couple of doors away, is a more casual spot where you get nibbles of the same to go with a nice glass of wine.

Eating

Manifesto   ITALIAN €€

3 🔪 MAP P138, A3

A table at this tiny Italian joint, which has a loyal legion of fans, is worth the wait. Pizzas are expertly charred with carefully curated toppings like tender-stem broccoli and Sicilian capers, and the wine list is inventive and vast, with a generous selection available by the glass. (📞01-496 8096; www. manifestorestaurant.ie; 208 Lower Rathmines Rd; pizzas €12-17, mains €19-25; ⏰5-10pm; 🚌14, 15, 140 from city centre)

Farmer Brown's   INTERNATIONAL €€

4 🔪 MAP P138, E1

The hicky-chic decor and mismatched furniture won't be to everyone's liking, but there's no disagreement about the food, which makes this spot our choice for best brunch in Dublin. From healthy smashed avocado to a stunning Cuban pork sandwich, it has all your lazy breakfast needs covered, and is very much worth the effort. There's another **branch** (📞086-046 8837; www.farmerbrowns. ie; 170 Lower Rathmines Rd; mains €16-28; ⏰10am-4pm & 5-10pm; 🚌14, 15 from city centre) in Rathmines. (📞01-660 2326; www.farmerbrowns. ie; 25A Bath Ave; brunch €7-12, dinner €15-28; ⏰10am-4pm & 5-8.30pm; 📶; 🚌7, 8 from city centre, 🚉Grand Canal Dock)

Little Mike's   SEAFOOD €€

5 🔪 MAP P138, E4

At Little Mike's, opened in 2019, you can sit at the counter for a few glasses of wine and some smaller plates of the seafood that Michael's, its sister restaurant, is known (and loved) for. A few doors down from Michael's, this spot is a more casual iteration. (www. littlemikes.ie; 63 Deerpark Rd; mains €15-32; ⏰noon-10pm Thu-Sun; 🚌47 from city centre)

Stella Diner

DINER €€

6 MAP P138, A4

Unsurprisingly, American comfort food is at the heart of this stylish spot, where diners tuck into hot dogs and burgers from red-leather booths. If you have a craving for American pancakes, these are some of the best in town — fluffy, light and accompanied by a generous jug of maple syrup. Unlimited filter coffee is a nice touch, too. (01-496 7063; www.stelladiner.ie; 211 Lower Rathmines Rd; mains €8-20; 8am-10pm; 14, 15, 140 from city centre)

Butcher Grill

INTERNATIONAL €€

7 MAP P138, C3

No surprise that this terrific spot specialises in meat, which is locally sourced and cooked to perfection in its wood-smoked grill. From venison to a superb *côte de boeuf* (rib steak) to share – there are few spots in town where the meat sweats are so welcome. The weekend roasts are top notch too, with duck fat roasties and Yorkshire pudding. (01-498 1805; www.the-butchergrill.ie; 92 Ranelagh Rd; mains €20-36; 5.30-9.30pm Sun-Wed, to 10.30pm Thu-Sat, plus noon-3.30pm Sat & Sun; Ranelagh)

The Northside & the Southside

It was traditionally assumed that the southside is totally posh and the northside is a derelict slum – at least before gentrification began transforming virtually the whole of the city centre. But while most of the city has been given the developer's lick of paint, attitudes about the city's various neighbourhoods remain entrenched.

The 'southside' generally refers to Dublin 4 and the fancy suburbs immediately west and south – conveniently ignoring the traditionally working-class neighbourhoods in southwestern Dublin such as Bluebell and Tallaght. North Dublin is huge, but the northside tag is usually applied to the inner suburbs, where incomes are typically lower, accents are more pronouncedly Dublin, and – most recently – the influx of foreign nationals is more in evidence.

All Dubliners are familiar with the 'posh twit' stereotype born and raised on the southside, but there's another kind of Dubliner, usually from the middle-class districts of northern Dublin, who affects a salt-of-the-earth accent while talking about the 'gee-gees' and says things like 'tis far from sushi we was rared' while tucking into a maki roll.

Chophouse GASTROPUB €€

8 MAP P138, E1

This fine sprawling bar is a terrific gastropub where the focus is on juicy cuts of steak. That said, reluctant carnivores also have a choice of fish, chicken or lamb dishes. It does an excellent Sunday lunch – the slow-braised pork belly is delicious. It's a popular watering hole when there's a match on at the Aviva Stadium (p143). (☑01-660 2390; www.thechophouse.ie; 2 Shelbourne Rd; lunch €15-25, dinner €16-35; ⊙restaurant noon-2.30pm & 6-10pm Mon-Fri, 5-10pm Sat, 1-8pm Sun; ☐4, 7, 8, 120 from city centre)

Drinking

Blackbird PUB

9 MAP P138, A3

Candelit and cosy, this boozer epitomises the new-style Irish pub, full of mismatching furniture, interesting curios and private snugs, with some retro video games thrown in. A good mix of traditional and craft drinks. (☑01-559 1940; www.facebook.com/BlackbirdRathmines; 82-84 Lower Rathmines Rd; ⊙4pm-midnight Mon-Thu & Sun, to 1am Fri & Sat; ☎; ☐14, 15, 140 from city centre)

Taphouse BAR

10 MAP P138, B3

Locals refer to it by its original name of Russell's, but that doesn't mean that the regulars aren't delighted with the new owners'

sprucing up of a village favourite. What they didn't change was the beloved balcony – the best spot in which to have a drink on a warm day. (☑01-491 3436; www.taphouse.ie; 60 Ranelagh Rd; ⊙12.30pm-11.30am Mon-Thu, to 12.30am Fri & Sat, to 11pm Sun; ☐Ranelagh)

Beggar's Bush PUB

11 MAP P138, D1

A staunch defender of the traditional pub aesthetic, Ryan's (as it's referred to by its older clientele) has adjusted to the modern age by adding an outside patio for good weather. Everything else, though, has remained the same, which is precisely why it's so popular with flat-capped pensioners and employees from nearby Google. (Jack Ryan's; www.beggarsbush.com; 115 Haddington Rd; ⊙10.30am-11pm Mon-Thu, to 12.30am Fri & Sat, 12.30-11pm Sun; ☐4, 7, 8, 120 from city centre, ☐Grand Canal Dock)

Entertainment

Stella Theatre CINEMA

12 MAP P138, A4

A cinema night may not always be a glamorous event, but at the Stella Theatre it is. A narrow entrance opens up to sumptuous art deco glory with comfortable leather seats paired with tables and footstools. Leave extra time to order food that will be delivered during the film, or book ahead to go to the cocktail club upstairs. (☑01-496 7014; www.stellatheatre.ie;

Royal Dublin Society Showground

207-209 Lower Rathmines Rd; tickets from €19; ⌚5pm-late Mon-Fri, from 9am Sat & Sun; 🚌14, 15, 140 from city centre)

Aviva Stadium
STADIUM

13 ⭐ MAP P138, E1

Gleaming 50,000-capacity ground with an eye-catching curvilinear stand in the swanky neighbourhood of Donnybrook. Home to Irish rugby and football internationals. (📞01-238 2300; www.avivastadium.ie; 11-12 Lansdowne Rd; 🚆Lansdowne Rd)

Royal Dublin Society Showground
SPECTATOR SPORT

14 ⭐ MAP P138, E3

This impressive, Victorian-era showground is used for various exhibitions throughout the year. The most important annual event here is the late-July **Dublin Horse Show**, which includes an international showjumping contest. Leinster rugby also plays its home matches in the 35,000-capacity arena. Ask at the tourist office for other events. (RDS Showground; 📞01-668 9878; www.rds.ie; Merrion Rd, Ballsbridge; 🚌7 from Trinity College)

Survival Guide

O'Connell Bridge over the Liffey PAWEL.GAUL/GETTY IMAGES ©

Before You Go

Book Your Stay

A relative lack of beds means hotel prices can skyrocket, particularly at weekends and during the high season (May to September). There are good midrange options north of the Liffey, but the biggest spread of accommodation is south of the river, from midrange Georgian townhouses to the city's top hotels. Budget travellers rely on the selection of decent hostels, many of which have private rooms as well as dorms.

Useful Websites

All Dublin Hotels (www.irelandhotels.com/hotels) Decent spread of accommodation in the city centre and suburbs.

Daft.ie (www.daft.ie) If you're looking to rent in Dublin, this is the site to search.

Dublin Hotels (www.dublinhotels.com)

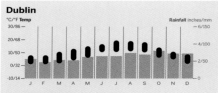

Dublin

°C/°F Temp   Rainfall inches/mm

When to Go

○ **May** Sees both rain and sun.

○ **Jun–Aug** Dublin weather at its best

○ **Sept** Can be warm and sunny.

○ **Nov–Feb** Cold but dry.

Hotels in the city centre and beyond.

Dublin Tourism (www.visitdublin.com) Good selection of rated accommodation.

Hostel Dublin (www.hosteldublin.com) Good info on hostels.

Lonely Planet (lonelyplanet.com/ireland/dublin/hotels) Expert recommendations.

Best Budget

Generator Hostel (www.staygenerator.com) Funky hostel on the north side.

Grafton Guesthouse (www.graftonguesthouse.com) Cool, lofty style in a gorgeous red-brick building.

Isaacs Hostel (www.isaacs.ie) Superb hostel

near Connolly Station.

Kelly's Hotel (www.kellysdublin.com) Minimalist boutique chic smack in the middle of the action.

Ariel House (www.ariel-house.net) Gorgeous southside B&B.

Best Midrange

Devlin Hotel (www.thedevlin.ie) Super-cool suburban hotel.

Cliff Townhouse (www.theclifftownhouse.com) Terrific boutique bolthole.

Brooks Hotel (www.brookshotel.ie) Welcoming and cosy, with an in-house cinema.

Aloft Dublin City (www.alofthotels.com) Amazing views from the rooftop terrace.

Number 31 (www.number31.ie) Stylish, modernist guesthouse.

Best Top End

Merrion (www.merrionhotel.com) Sophisticated, elegant and central.

Shelbourne (www.theshelbourne.ie) A Dublin institution.

Conrad Dublin (www.conradhotels.com) Superb, modern rooms.

Westbury (www.doylecollection.com) Can't get more central.

Marker (www.themarkerhoteldublin.com) Architectural elegance.

Arriving in Dublin

Dublin Airport

Dublin Airport (☎ 01-814 1111; www.dublinairport.com) is 13km north of the city centre and has two terminals: most international flights (including most US flights) use Terminal 2; Ryanair and select others use Terminal 1. Both terminals have the usual selection of pubs, restaurants, shops, ATMs and car-hire desks.

Aircoach (☎ 01-844 7118; www.aircoach.ie; one way/return €7/10) Private coach service with three routes from the airport to more than 20 destinations throughout the city, including the main streets of the city centre. Coaches run every 10 to 15 minutes between 6am and midnight, then hourly from midnight to 6am.

Dublin Bus (www.dodublin.ie; 59 Upper O'Connell St; adult/child €27/12; ☉ 10.30am daily May-Sep, 10.30am Mon, Fri & Sat Apr, Oct & Nov, 10.30am Fri & Sat Mar) A number of buses serve the airport from various points in Dublin, including buses 16 (Rathfarnham), 41 (Lower Abbey St) and 102 (Sutton/Howth); all cross the city centre on their way to the airport.

Taxi There is a taxi rank directly outside the arrivals concourse of both terminals. It should take about 45 minutes to get into the city centre by taxi, and cost around €25, including an initial charge of €3.80 (€4.20 between 10pm and 8am and on Sundays and bank holidays). Ensure the meter is on.

Dublin Port Terminal

The **Dublin Port Terminal** (☎ 01-855 2222; Alexandra Rd; 🚌 53 from Talbot St) is 3km northeast of the city centre.

Bus An express bus transfer service to and from Dublin Port is operated by **Morton's Bus** (www.mortonscoaches.ie; adult/child €3.50/2; ☉ 7.15am, 12.30pm, 2pm & 7pm), leaving from Westmoreland St and timed to coincide with ferry departures. Otherwise, regular bus 53 serves the port from Talbot St. Inbound ferries are met by timed bus services that run to the city centre.

Getting Around

Bicycle

○ **Dublinbikes** (www.dublinbikes.ie), a public bicycle-rental scheme with more than 100 stations spread across the city centre.

o Purchase a €5 three-day card (as well as paying a credit-card deposit of €150) online or at select stations where credit cards can be used.

o You'll be issued a ticket with an ID and PIN that you'll need to free a bike for use, which is then free of charge for the first 30 minutes and €0.50 for each half-hour thereafter.

o There is a (growing) network of cycle lanes, but encroachment by larger vehicles such as buses and trucks is a major problem in the city centre, so you'll have to keep your wits about you.

Bus

o Buses run from around 6am (some start at 5.30am) to about 11.30pm. **Dublin Bus** (☎01-873 4222; www.dublinbus.ie; 59 Upper O'Connell St; �l9am-5.30pm Tue-Fri, to 2pm Sat, 8.30am-5.30pm Mon; ☐all city centre) has a free app for all its services.

o Fares are calculated according to stages (stops): from €2.15 (one to three stages) to €3.30 (more than 13 stages).

If paying cash, you must tender exact change.

o A Leap Card (www.leapcard.ie), available from most newsagents, is 20% cheaper than cash fares.

o Nitelink late-night services (€6.60; €4.50 with Leap Card) run every 20 minutes from the city centre on Fridays and Saturdays; see www.dublinbus.ie for route details.

Car & Motorcycle

o Traffic in Dublin is a nightmare and parking can be an expensive headache.

o There's no free parking anywhere in the city centre during business hours (7am to 7pm from Monday to Saturday), but there is plenty of paid parking, priced according to zone: €2.90 per hour in the yellow (central) zone down to €0.60 in the blue (suburban).

o Supervised and sheltered car parks cost around €4 per hour, with most offering a low-cost evening flat rate.

o Clamped illegally parked cars incur an €80 charge for removal.

o Parking is free after 7pm Monday to Saturday, and all day Sunday, in most metered spots (unless indicated) and on single yellow lines.

o All the main agencies are at the airport and in the city centre, including **Avis Rent-a-Car** (☎01-605 7500; www.avis.ie; 35 Old Kilmainham Rd; �l9.30am-5.45pm Mon-Fri, to 2.30pm Sat & Sun; ☐23, 25, 25A, 26, 68, 69 from city centre), **Budget Rent-a-Car** (☎ 01-837 9611; www.budget.ie; 151 Lower Drumcondra Rd; �l99am-6pm; ☐41 from O'Connell St), **Europcar** (☎01-812 2800; www.europcar.ie; 1 Mark St; �l98am-6pm Mon-Fri, 8.30am-3pm Sat & Sun; ☐all city centre), **Hertz Rent-a-Car** (☎ 01-709 3060; www.hertz.com; 151 S Circular Rd; �l98.30am-5.30pm Mon-Fri, 9am-4.30pm Sat, 9am-3.30pm Sun; ☐9, 16, 77, 79 from city centre) and **Thrifty** (☎01-844 1944; www.thrifty.ie; 26 E Lombard St; �l98am-6pm Mon-Fri, to 3pm Sat & Sun; ☐all city centre).

Tram

o The Luas (www.luas.ie) light-rail system has two lines: the Green Line (every five to 15 minutes) from Broombridge in the north of the city down through O'Connell St and St Stephen's Green to Sandyford in south Dublin (via Ranelagh and Dundrum); and the Red Line (every 20 minutes) from the Point Village to Tallaght via the north quays and Heuston Station.

o There are ticket machines at every stop or you can use a tap-on, tap-off Leap Card, which is available from most newsagents. A typical short-hop fare (around four stops) is €2.80. Services run from 5.30am to 12.30am Monday to Friday, from 6.30am to 12.30am Saturday and from 7am to 11.30pm Sunday.

Train

o The **Dublin Area Rapid Transport** (DART; ☏ 01-836 6222; www. irishrail.ie) provides quick train access to the coast as far north as Howth (about 30 minutes) and as far south as Greystones in County Wicklow. Pearse Station is convenient for central Dublin south of the Liffey, and Connolly

Fare-Saver Passes

Fare-saver passes include the following:

DoDublin Card (adult/child €35/10) Three-day unlimited travel on all bus services, including Airlink and Dublin Bus hop-on, hop-off tours as well as entry to the Little Museum of Dublin and a walking tour.

Luas Flexi Ticket (1/7/30 days from €7/16.50/66) Unlimited travel on all Luas services. The one-day pass covers all zones; the multiday passes start at one zone.

Rambler Pass (5/30 days €33/165) Valid for unlimited travel on all Dublin Bus and Airlink services, except Nitelink.

Visitor Leap Card (1/3/7 days €10/19.50/40) Unlimited travel on bus, Luas and DART, including Airlink, Nitelink and Xpresso buses.

Station for north of the Liffey.

o There are services every 10 to 20 minutes, sometimes more frequently, from around 6.30am to midnight Monday to Saturday. Services are less frequent on Sunday.

Taxi

o All taxi fares begin with a flagfall of €3.80 (€4.20 from 10pm to 8am), followed by €1.14/0.40 per kilometre/minute thereafter (€1.50/0.53 from 10pm to 8am). Extra charges include €1 for each extra passenger

and €2 for telephone bookings. There is no charge for luggage.

o Taxis can be hailed on the street and found at taxi ranks around the city, including on the corner of Abbey and O'Connell Sts; College Green, in front of Trinity College; and St Stephen's Green at the end of Grafton St.

o Numerous taxi companies, such as **National Radio Cabs** (☏ 01-677 2222; www.nrc.ie), dispatch taxis by radio. You can also try MyTaxi (www.mytaxi.com), a taxi app.

Essential Information

Accessible Travel

Dublin's compact city centre is mostly flat, with a few cobbled areas and a relatively accessible public-transport network, making it an attractive destination for people with mobility issues. While most DART stations are accessible, DART and train services require 24 hours' notice before boarding with a wheelchair. All city buses are wheelchair-accessible, but Luas offers maximum accessibility.

Resources

Download Lonely Planet's free Accessible Travel guides from http://lptravel.to/AccessibleTravel.

Accessible Ireland (www.accessibleireland.com) Reviews, plus short introductions to public transport.

Ireland.com (www.ireland.com/en-us/accommodation/

articles/accessibility) Informative article with links to accessibility information for transport and tourist attractions.

Irish Wheelchair Association (📞 01-818 6400; www.iwa.ie) Useful national association.

Mobility Mojo (www.mobilitymojo.com) It has more than 500 reviews of establishments in a searchable database, mostly in Dublin and Galway but expanding all the time.

Trip-Ability (www.trip-ability.com) Review site that should soon feature a booking facility.

Business Hours

Standard opening hours in relatively late-rising Dublin are as follows:

Banks 10am to 4pm Monday to Wednesday and Friday, 10am to 5pm Thursday

Offices 9am to 5pm Monday to Friday

Post Offices 9am to 6pm Monday to Friday, 9am to 1pm Saturday

Restaurants noon to 10pm (or midnight); food service generally ends around 9pm; top-

end restaurants often close 3pm to 6pm; restaurants serving brunch open around 11am

Shops 9.30am to 6pm Monday to Wednesday, Friday and Saturday, 9.30am to 8pm Thursday (to 9pm for bigger shopping centres and supermarkets), noon to 6pm Sunday

Discount Cards

Senior citizens are entitled to discounts on public transport and museum fees. Students and under-26s also get discounts with the appropriate student or youth card. Local discount passes include the following:

Dublin Pass (adult/child one-day €62/33, three-day €92/49) For heavy-duty sightseeing, the Dublin Pass will save you a packet. It provides free entry to over 25 attractions (including the Guinness Storehouse), discounts at 20 others and guaranteed fast-track entry to some of the busiest sights. To avail of the free Aircoach transfer to and from the airport, download the app before you arrive. Otherwise, it's available from any

Discover Ireland Dublin Tourism Centre.

Heritage Card
(adult/child/student €40/10/10) This card entitles you to free access to all sights in and around Dublin managed by the Office of Public Works (OPW). You can buy it at OPW sites or Dublin Tourism offices.

Electricity

**Type G
230V/50Hz**

Emergencies

Ambulance, Fire, Police (Gardai), Boat or Coastal Rescue	☎999 or 112
Rape Crisis Centre	☎1800 778 888
Country Code	☎353
International Access Code	☎00

LGBTIQ+ Travellers

Dublin is a pretty good place to be LGBTIQ+. Being gay or lesbian in the city is completely unremarkable, while in recent years members of the trans community have also found greater acceptance. However, LGBTIQ+ people can still be harrassed or worse, so if you do encounter any sort of trouble, call the **Crime Victims Helpline** (☎116006; ⊙24hr) or the **Sexual Assault Investigation Unit** (☎01-666 3430; www.garda.ie; ⊙24hr).

Resources include the following:

Gaire (www.gaire.com) Online message board and resource centre.

Gay Men's Health Project (☎01-660 2189; www.hse.ie/go/GMHS) Practical advice on men's health issues.

National LGBT Federation (☎01-675 5025; www.nxf.ie; 2 Upper Exchange St, Temple Bar; ⊙all city centre) Publishers of *Gay Community News*.

Outhouse (☎01-873 4932; www.outhouse.ie; 105 Capel St; ⊙10am–

6pm Mon-Fri, noon-5pm Sat; ⊙all city centre) Top LGBTIQ+ resource centre, and a great stop-off point to see what's on, check noticeboards and meet people. It publishes the free *Ireland's Pink Pages*, a directory of gay-centric services, also accessible on the website.

Money

ATMs are widespread. Credit cards (with PIN) are widely accepted in restaurants, hotels and shops.

ATMs

Most banks have ATMs that are linked to international money systems such as Cirrus, Maestro or Plus. Each transaction incurs a currency conversion fee, and credit cards can incur immediate and exorbitant cash-advance interest-rate charges. Also it is strongly recommended that if you're staying in the city centre, you get your money out early on a Friday to avoid the long queues that can form after 8pm.

Money-Saving Tips

o If you're going to use public transport, be sure to get a Leap Card (from most convenience stores): it's cheaper and much easier than cash.

o Lunch deals and pre-theatre menus are the best way to enjoy fine dining, even in the very best restaurants in town.

Changing Money

The best exchange rates are at banks, although bureaux de change and other exchange facilities usually open for longer hours. There's a cluster of banks located around College Green opposite Trinity College and all have currency exchange facilities.

Credit Cards

Visa and MasterCard credit and debit cards are widely accepted in Dublin. Smaller businesses prefer debit cards (and will charge a fee for credit cards). Nearly all credit and debit cards use the chip-and-PIN system, and an increasing number of places won't accept your card if you don't have your PIN.

Tipping

You're not obliged to tip if the service or food was unsatisfactory.

Hotels Only for bellhops who carry luggage, then €1 per bag.

Pubs Not expected unless table service is provided, then €1 for a round of drinks.

Restaurants Tip 10% for decent service, up to 15% in more expensive places.

Taxis Tip 10% or round up to the nearest euro.

Toilet attendants Tip €0.50.

Public Holidays

Christmas Day is the only day on the calendar when all pubs close. Otherwise, the half-dozen or so bank holidays (most of which fall on a Monday) mean just that – the banks are closed, along with about half the shops. St Patrick's Day and St Stephen's Day holidays are taken on the following Monday should they fall on a weekend.

New Year's Day
1 January

St Patrick's Day
17 March

Easter (Good Friday to Easter Monday inclusive) March/April

May Bank Holiday
First Monday in May

June Bank Holiday
First Monday in June

August Bank Holiday
First Monday in August

October Bank Holiday
Last Monday in October

Christmas Day
25 December

St Stephen's Day
26 December

Safe Travel

Dublin is a safe city by any standards, except maybe those set by the Swiss. Basically, act as you would at home.

o Don't leave anything visible in your car when you park.

- Skimming at ATMs is an ongoing problem; be sure to cover the keypad with your hand when you input your PIN.

- Take care around the western edge of Thomas St (onto James St), where drug addicts are often present.

- The northern end of Gardiner St and the areas northeast of there have crime-related problems.

- You'll need a face mask, ID and your Covid-19 vaccine pass for many indoor establishments, including restaurants, bars, cafes and cinemas.

- Many museums and organised events require pre-booking to control numbers.

Police Stations

Police stations are located in the following areas:

Docklands (01-677 8141; Pearse St; all city centre)

Merrion Sq area (01-676 3481; Harcourt Tce; 24hr; Harcourt)

North of the Liffey (Store St; Connolly) Plus another **east of**

Mountjoy Sq (Fitzgibbon St; 122 from city centre).

Telephone Services

All European and Australasian mobile phones work in Dublin, as do North American phones not locked to a local network. Check with your provider. Prepaid SIM cards start from €20.

Toilets

There are no on-street facilities in Dublin. All shopping centres have public toilets; if you're stranded, go into any bar or hotel.

Tourist Information

Visit Dublin Centre (www.visitdublin.com; 25 Suffolk St; 9am-5.30pm Mon-Sat, 10.30am-3pm Sun; all city centre) General visitor information on Dublin and Ireland, as well as an accommodation and booking service.

Visas

Not required for citizens of Australia, New Zealand, the USA or Canada, or citizens

of European nations that belong to the European Economic Area (EEA).

Responsible Travel

Overtourism

- Visit in the off-season: Pre-pandemic, Dublin welcomed nine million visitors, most of whom came between May and September. Off-season visits are less crowded, hotel rates are usually cheaper and you're more likely to have a more authentic experience.

- Linger longer: You'll need more than a day to get the best out of Dublin. Beyond the major highlights are fascinating museums and wonderful day trips to seaside villages and mountains.

- Stay in registered accommodation. Unlicensed accommodation providers have been a scourge, driving up rental prices that have priced many out completely.

Support Local & Give Back

o Buy discounted food that would otherwise be thrown out from restaurants signed up to the Too Good To Go (toogoodtogo.ie) app.

o Support restaurateurs and retailers affiliated with Support Dublin (www.supportdublin. com), set up during the pandemic as a way

of supporting local businesses affected by Covid-19.

o Some of the most eye-opening tours of Dublin are the **Secret Street Tours** (www.secret streettours.org) led by former rough sleepers, which offer an unforgettable insight into Dublin's streets from those who once lived and slept on them. All profits go towards

o charities that support the homeless.

Leave a Light Footprint

o One of the most popular ways to get around the city is with the blue bikes of **dublinbikes** (www.dublinbikes.ie), a public bicycle-rental scheme with more than 100 stations spread across the city centre.

Behind the Scenes

Send Us Your Feedback

We love to hear from travellers – your comments help make our books better. We read every word, and we guarantee that your feedback goes straight to the authors. Visit **lonelyplanet.com/contact** to submit your updates and suggestions.

Note: We may edit, reproduce and incorporate your comments in Lonely Planet products such as guidebooks, websites and digital products, so let us know if you don't want your comments reproduced or your name acknowledged. For a copy of our privacy policy visit lonelyplanet.com/privacy.

Fionn's Thanks

Dublin's forever changing, and to update it properly I need more than two eyes and one brain, so a huge thanks to everyone who helped me along. To the staff in the Dublin office, thanks for your tips, suggestions and recommendations; to Nicola Brady, for her invaluable assistance in knowing all of the right places to eat; and to Cliff Wilkinson, the ever-present, ever-helpful editor who answered all of my questions.

Acknowledgements

Cover photograph: Trinity College (p36), David Soanes/ Shutterstock ©

Back cover photograph: Kilmainham Gaol (p96), matthi/ Shutterstock ©

Photographs pp30–31 (left to right): Popa Ioana Mirela; Gabriela Insuratelu; faithie/Shutterstock ©

This Book

This 6th edition of Lonely Planet's *Pocket Dublin* guidebook was researched and written by Fionn Davenport, who also wrote the previous two editions. This guidebook was produced by the following:

Destination Editor Clifton Wilkinson

Senior Product Editors Sandie Kestell, Jessica Ryan

Product Editors Pete Cruttenden, Shona Gray

Senior Cartographer Mark Griffiths

Assisting Cartographers Alison Lyall, Julie Sheridan

Book Designers Fergal Condon, Lauren Egan

Assisting Editors Andrew Bain, Imogen Bannister, Nigel Chin, Carly Hall, Victoria Harrison, Kellie Langdon, Rosie Nicholson, Kristin Odijk, Simon Williamson

Cover Researchers Meri Blazevski, Gwen Cotter

Thanks to Alex Conroy Kate James, Sonia Kapoor, Kate Kiely, Angela Tinson, Juan Winata

Index

See also separate subindexes for:

- ⊗ **Eating** p158
- ⊙ **Drinking** p159
- ✪ **Entertainment** p159
- ⊙ **Shopping** p159